In India: Everything is Sunshine and Rainbows!

In India: Everything is Sunshine and Rainbows!

Anushray Singh

ZB

ZORBA BOOKS

ZORBA BOOKS

Published in India by Zorba Books, 2018

Website: www.zorbabooks.com
Email: info@zorbabooks.com

Copyright © Anushray Singh

ISBN Print Book - 978-93-87456-14-3

Zorba Books Pvt. Ltd.(opc)
Gurgaon, INDIA

Printed at Repro Knowledgecast Limited, Thane

This book is dedicated to my family and especially my mother for being a rock steady figure in my life. I would like to thank everyone and anyone who has been kind, caring and supportive of me. I like to believe kindness is the greatest virtue of humanity and even a stranger's kindness can motivate you to do great things.

"Patriotism cannot be our final spiritual shelter;
my refuge is humanity. I will not buy glass for the
price of diamonds, and I will never allow patriotism
to triumph over humanity as long as I live."

—*Rabindranath Tagore*

"For great men, religion is a way of making friends;
small people make religion a fighting tool."

—*A.P.J. Abdul Kalam*

Contents

Preface   xi
In India: Everything is Sunshine and Rainbows!   xiii

The Indian Way of Things

1. Why do Indians lack social etiquette and civic sense?   3
2. Indian roads are the places where most
    Indianness can be seen!   7
3. Not in my Backyard   16
4. The Toilet Conundrum   19
5. Are we ignorant of racism in India?   22
6. Why foreign tourists find their
    Indian experience as bittersweet?   25
7. The Indian Language Conundrum   30
8. What instigates communal riots?   33
9. Sports and India   38
10. Beggars of India: Theatrical tragedy?   41
11. The Curious Case of Mental Health in India   43
12. LGBT and India   45
13. Film industry of our country   49
14. Indian Television Industry   52
15. Offence R Us   55
16. Religion > Logic   59
17. We wait until the problem gets even bigger   63
18. Cringeworthy News Channels   65

The Peculiar Indian Society

1. The '*Chalta hai*' attitude of the Indian society   73
2. '*Log kya kahenge*' doesn't really make much sense   76

3. Coaching Classes and Mass Production of Engineers 79
4. Student suicide: Two words that shouldn't be used
    in the same sentence   84
5. The Narrative of Elitism and 'Gawar'   88
6. When Profession decides your Social Worth!   91
7. The Indian Arranged Marriage Network   94
8. Is Dowry in India, a mere gift exchanging custom? 97
9. Boys will be Boys   99
10. Online Harassment and Trolls   101
11. Love in India only looks good on silver screen   104
12. Feminism, Misandry and Patriarchy   106
13. The Godmen Epidemic   109

The Flailing Indian Machinery

1. Superiority complex of the Police,
    Bureaucrats and Elected Representatives   115
2. We are not subjects of a Monarch   117
3. Nepotism in India is an age-old concept: 119
4. The Mediocrity and Inefficiency of Our Government 121
5. Corruption and India   123
6. The Dying 'Nyaypalika' of this Country   127
7. Journalism and India   129
8. Are we a country of hurt sentiments?   131
9. Left and right in Indian context   135
10. Extreme Right, Polarization and Indian constitution 138
11. Epidemic of Fake News and Political Trolls   140

Epilogue
Armchair activism, shedding jingoism and
vision for India   142

Preface

Before we begin, let me clarify my intention. This book is an attempt to present a collection of shortcomings that had and has been hindering India's progress both philosophically and morally. Here, I am not trying to be a pseudo-intellectual, social justice warrior or a cynic, but rather trying to share my views that hopefully might lead to a constructive discussion or just present an outlook that the reader can relate to or empathise with. The book is not about properly calculated solutions or as a matter of fact, it isn't talking about specific problems; the book is rather an observation on the society. I feel that our country has been ignoring a wide range of issues and as a citizen who gets deeply affected by these, I intend to discuss about them by bringing forth my take on the issues. Through this book, I want to engage you in a debate or a discussion that will make you think hard and might also shift your moral compass. I have used metaphors and jokes in between harsh rants to inspire ridicule and bring out the best possible narration of the current situation that we are living in. If you are among the ones who get easily offended, then this book might not tickle your funny bone. If you are a level-headed human being who can weigh one man's opinions to yours and come to your own conclusion, then you are the one that this book has been written for.

I have presented a viewpoint from the perspective of a young educated Indian. We know where different spectrums of journalists stand; we know where different politicians stand; we know about many factions of society stand; but do we know or honestly care about the stance of the educated youth? I am talking about a young population that is highest in terms of number in this world yet struggling to get their voice heard.

Now, to be more specific, the book is not a cynical pessimistic cry or banter of some sort. It is a rant and even a satire at times - where you can sense the comical ironies and the frustrations of the writer. It's ranting because it doesn't have a specific structure or a formal approach, but is a collection of personal viewpoints often backed by facts. It's not banter because it isn't some light hearted joke or internet troll. The book is honest to its core and understands that some might not agree with the content it carries but in all fairness, the book respects your viewpoints. So it asks 'you', the reader to not get offended by it, rather be receptive of it. The book might open up a dialogue or it might not even be concrete enough to stir up anything, but at least it's talking about the things that need to be talked about; let these pages be a small drop in a sea of diverse voices and opinions that is, what I believe, the beauty of my country India.

Let's begin with this wonderful quote by George Washington,

"If freedom of speech is taken away then dumb and silent we may be led, like sheep to the slaughter."

In India: Everything is Sunshine and Rainbows!

Everyone has opinions, but the problem is that some opinions are based on botched-up biases, stereotypes and straight out lies that can be destructive. Now, there are other opinions based on facts, true to its core but bitter to swallow. But as humans we love the sweet sensation rather than a bitter one, so we tend to accept what is known as the 'twisted truth' which is formed just to sweeten the bitter taste of reality. The world is created on all these lies which have somehow passed as truth to create a state of hypernormalisation. This term is made relevant by the famous British documentary maker 'Adam Curtis'; he speaks about how harsh realities are accepted as the new normal or rather thrust into public consciousness to be seen as a very normal affair (which it is not). India has made peace with the idea of hypernormalisation - we see all the evil around us, yet we have somehow normalised it and made peace with it.

The rampant poverty in every nook and corner is overshadowed by claims of one of the fastest growing economy or even by one or two skyscrapers in one or two metropolises; the corrupt government's sins are always forgotten when they do one right thing after thousand blunders; the fact that we as a country, lack basic facilities like water, sanitation, food and electricity is overshadowed by the examples of one or two rural areas that has made progress; there are many such discussions later in the book that talk about how India accepts small victories and rides high on one or two good examples and conveniently forgets the overwhelming plethora of problems. The fault is not ours but of the ones calling the shots (government), the one who bankrolls them (the rich) and their voice boxes (the media). For starters the politicians don't care about all the problems; for them some problems are required to be squeezed until all the votes trickle down from them; their banks support them with their narrow and focused agendas of control and then comes the media who just care more for sensationalism than serious journalism. The media operates on two spectrums — either taking a very effective pro stance or an extremely opposite stance. Now, we all know that everyone wants to revel in the wave of optimism and thus we get high hopes that now our country will be the best in all spheres, we will beat China in terms of economic growth, we are just there with the US and European elites and then there is this weird superiority complex of Indian culture being the best in the world. Politician hide under the notion that India doesn't have any real problem.

Now, people often tend to misconstrue ranting; some believe that it is someone complaining about his/her surroundings for too long or from the perspective of a grossly stupid optimist, ranting is unnecessary as ignoring the wrong is right because everything around us is just sunshine and rainbows.

In our country, the philosophy of everything being sunshine and rainbow is quite predominant. Poverty, hunger, corruption, crime, injustice and brutality are all around, yet very few people feel the need to call a spade a spade, while the others will go on calling their country greatest, with unmatched culture, heritage and tradition. Yes, I do get the emotion behind it, and heck I love my country dearly but let's not put our historical significance or our cultural heritage as gigantic covers for all that is inherently bad. There are numerous things that make our country great – diversity, cultural significance and a heritage so unique that its identity is unparalleled to anyone else in the world.

I assure that the book does not record inaccurate opinions or something that anyone living in India hadn't felt or experienced. A healthy criticism must always be welcomed, it doesn't mean that I intend to disrespect my country, but it is an honest account of what is wrong around us. Criticising one's country doesn't mean you are an anti-nationalist; let it be considered as the first step of establishing oneself as a free-spirited citizen who wants to bring out the loopholes in daylight and not hide it in dark, ignorant corners.

This sentiment that our country is the best and if you dare say anything in contradiction, you are the 'enemy' is indeed bizarre. It is such an effective cover up by the ones in power, that laymen in India are somehow convinced that our culture, languages and traditions is the best in the world; now what this narcissistic and ignorant sentiment does is cut every problem that some tradition and custom puts forward. On the other side, any form of social change also gets halted by this ideology that you shouldn't change what is clearly the best culture in the world. Now because of this very weird belief of being the best culture in the world, we have inherited the worst problems of the world as well, namely poverty, hunger, caste bias, racism, religious tensions, inept governance, patriarchy etc. We might claim confidently that our culture is better than the countries in the West but then how come they are more developed and successful, while we are still struggling with very basic problems? No one has an answer. It's best to say that there is sunshine everywhere and rainbows sprouting from every Indian mouth.

The government is very clever — they know that this country has a habit of defending some of its nonsensical traditions and customs with rage and fury — thus politician go on to different people — either fanning the fire or pandering to them. Everyone knows how archaic cultural norms are pushing this country backwards, yet we as a country, drunk in our past greatness and ignorance are suffering and hurting. The country has every right to be proud of her culture and identity, but it doesn't have the right to be ignorant of its greatness, she shouldn't chide other country's culture who are clearly more successful than her.

This book aims to remove the rose-tinted glasses that showcase our country in the light of exaggerated greatness and bring forth the reality; do appreciate our country's gems and do criticize it's filth; do encourage the cultural inheritance but discourage the bigoted and archaic customs of the past; do follow your tradition but don't narcissistically think that yours is the best in the world.

In India or even in the rest of the world, sunshine and rainbows are rare, and claiming their presence everywhere is stupid and foolish. India and Indians face problems that are so bizarre and unique that almost no other country (apart from the other less developed neighbouring Asian countries) seems to relate. We have third world problems of poverty, hunger and water; we have weird cultural issues and deep racial divide; we have social, economic and political problems, and I, for once, would like to talk about them with strong of hope of opening a constructive discussion rather than shallow social media venting and news anchors shouting on top of their lungs.

The Indian Way of Things

Why do Indians lack
social etiquette and civic sense?

We, Indians are the worst in empathising. The country, overran by a huge population (almost 1.3 billion) has failed to teach her citizens how to grasp the meaning of empathy towards their fellow countrymen. In India, people would push and pull, misbehave and indulge in various social faux pas. It's so evident to see the gaps in our social etiquettes, when compared to a good percentage of the world. We don't care about each other, we just have this habit of getting our self-interest fulfilled and shun out the interest of others. I am not exaggerating how 'we' Indians give no damns to the concept of social etiquette. No one teaches us and if someone preaches etiquette to us, we lose our cool. That's precisely why we need civic sense as a subject in schools and colleges.

Have you ever been to a crowded Indian market or travelled in any Indian public transport? Isn't it a lovely experience? All forms of social etiquette goes down the goddamn drain. People just go berserk when they see crowd. People would let their limbs go loose when they want to get either on a bus or a train or a share-auto or a metro; these limbs can be hurled towards you and when I say you, it could be a little girl or an elderly person; these limbs wouldn't hesitate for a second. People in India are always in a hurry; they just need to thrust themselves in a crowd. You might say that this is prevalent amongst people who are uneducated or are from rural areas where etiquettes are a lost cause. My friend, you are wrong. Let me give you an example of how social etiquette is absent in both the educated and uneducated sections of our country. Have you ever travelled by air domestically in India? Majority of its travellers, I assume are the so-called educated class of this society. The moment the flight lands and the seatbelt signal goes off, people lose their mind collectively. It takes about 5-10 minutes before the plane door opens. Here, social etiquette dictates that one should wait and remain seated until the airhost/hostess instructs that you can now exit. You are supposed to then rise from your seat, politely get your hand baggage from the overhead compartment and help others by giving their luggage if it's in your vicinity. Then you must walk patiently in a queue and get out of the plane. Now, this never happens when the flight is boarded by Indians. They would just rise emphatically from their seats, creating chaos in the narrow lane between the seats; they would try to get their luggage from the above compartment so inconveniently that it would often hit other passengers who are already struggling for space in that tightly squeezed lane. Now, people get their hand baggage after tussling with fellow passengers — like sheep in a herd — they would stand for five minutes in a crowded mob in that narrow airplane aisle. Why can't we just wait until the plane's door opens? Why can't we just let the aisle passengers get up first, followed by the passengers in the middle seat and then the last set of passengers seating on the window seats?

People in India collectively have shunned civic sense and social etiquettes. The main reason is that the population is so humongous that, we, as a society have least respect for people around us. Secondly, we Indians are brought up with a mentality that we have to survive in this country by struggling rather than live co-operatively. People in planes, trains and buses play music loudly, talk loudly with each other or over their phones and take up extra amount of spaces, not giving a damn about the fellow passengers. In India, either we are ambivalent about other people's comfort or are just too self-centred to think of one's comfort. People listening to loud music (not giving a single damn about the fellow passengers), sitting on floors of a public transport, talking loudly, smelling badly and thrusting armpits on people around by being oblivious to one's body odour and the social etiquette violation list goes on. We have accepted this as normal behaviour. You have to deal with the same type of ordeal whether you travel by train or bus or even flights.

The beauty here is that if you try to confront any of these morons, you will find yourself in a weird squabble, because the one you are pointing your finger at is ignorant of any form of mistake on his/her part; now you would assume that people around you who were also suffering due to that moron's actions and would jump in and help you. Here in majority of the cases, the Indian crowd would stay mum and would stand idle witnessing the drama. People in India would just watch people fight; they would watch a man bleed to death and would have the audacity to video record it but won't take action; they would watch people suffering in a road accident where a crowd would gather around and no one will do anything. In India, we just have made peace with the fact that there is lack of social etiquettes. We have made peace with a mentality that if you go outside in a public sphere, we have to switch on the survival mode and not give a shit about anyone else. We don't see people as people for most of the time; we are so self-centred as a country and we don't give a damn about grievances caused to others by our actions. People will park their cars in the middle of the street according to their convenience; people would urinate, defecate and spit on roads, walls and railway tracks; people in India would do an innumerable number of things that would cause grievances to their fellow citizens. This creates a cycle of frustration, where 'you', even being a smart, educated and responsible citizen of this country would eventually give in and start participating in a culture that clearly lacks civic sense and social etiquette.

Again, I have to say that this is not generalising. I get that there is a sizeable population that sees this as a major problem, and in a way are trying to showcase social etiquettes in an individual capacity. But we all know that the majority of people in this country showcase the worst form behaviour in a public sphere and this is something, we as a country have been failing to acknowledge. Many foreigners who visit India find it extremely shocking that a country with such beautiful history, tradition and hospitality customs, is so bad in social etiquettes. It boggles them that how can 'we' be like this, and to them this is a major problem; why aren't we talking about this weird attitude wherein a public sphere, Indians don't have the right amount of education of proper civil conduct.

I have been talking about civic sense, social etiquette and conduct which was directed domestically; now let's move this discussion in another direction. Foreigners who visit our country have both an amazing as well as horrible experience here in India. First of all, the people in this country haven't gotten sober from the colonial hangover. They still subconsciously believe anyone with white skin is more superior to them. Foreigners with fair skin find that they become an object of admiration — they get stared at, asked for pictures and even get harassed in the process. Any white tourist would feel like a rockstar in India. It's a mixture of Indian inferiority complex, where white skin is seen as superior (we'll talk about this in detail later ahead). People who come from outside aren't accustomed to the idea that we have somehow managed to make peace with and that is our horrible social conduct and the general chaos all around us.

I believe for a country to become great it needs more than just great infrastructure, booming economy and good governance; it needs a deep-rooted feeling in its population to be of a high moral and social character and sadly, we as a country lack that morality and frankly we don't give a shit about it.

Indian roads are the places where most Indianness can be seen!

When you step out of your house, you see the sun is shining, the birds are chirping and the wind caressing your hair. *Carpe Diem* which translates to 'seize the day'. Now you get inside your car and drive it further down your house, and at no more than sixty seconds, you see some moron trying to pull off something moronic on the roads. After almost five minutes and after encountering more than hundred road safety violations and moronic pedestrian acts, the sun doesn't feel to be shining that bright.

India can sometimes be called a beautiful chaos – an amalgamation of different cultures that are living together. But to say Indian roads to be beautiful chaos is very silly on our part. It's evident that the famous saying, "When in Rome, do what the Romans do!" is applicable to India in every possible way. Hey, you know all about the traffic rules and I also heard that you know the meaning of all the traffic signs – now that's all good and jolly – but just bundle up all this saintly traffic wisdom throw it out of your car's window because once you drive in an Indian road, then boy you would curse yourself for being a driver who abides by the traffic rules and isn't an inconsiderate jackass out on the roads.

If you try to be a good citizen out here in India – the country won't reward you for it – as opposed to being an inconsiderate schmuck that just works out perfectly here – take the bright shining examples of our politicians. Lord knows that I have tried to be a good driver following all the traffic rules and safety precautions and where did it land me? Nowhere. People honked at me because I stopped at a red light. How crazy of me to stop at a red light! There were cars that came in front of me when I drove on a green light. This had me confused, did I get my red and green light interpretation wrong?

Let's leave the vehicular menace for a moment and point our fingers at the wonderful pedestrians. They won't walk on the paths meant for pedestrians, they are adventurer and part-time adrenaline junkies, who get their thrills by crossing the roads when they can clearly see that there are cars and bikes running on the roads at high speed and even a ricochet with a high-speed vehicle will send them flying for miles but still they'll do what they please. The most baffling thing is that they have the audacity to show you – the driver – a hand like a traffic policeman – instructing you to hit brakes because it would be inconvenient for them to wait just a few minutes until the traffic stops and they can cross the roads. It happens everywhere in India – you witness the green light and you accelerate your car and suddenly this hand appears out of thin air instructing you to stop and let these adrenaline junkies cross the roads. I get it that you are an inconsiderate fool who doesn't give a damn about your own life and others out there on the road but the most astonishing part is that they are partaking this with their children in their arms sometimes. Be a moron yourself but don't let these little children be part of this moronic endeavour of yours. A person in India will only strap his/her seatbelt while driving if he/she spots a policeman ahead on the road. Safety of one's life is not important but the thought that a policeman would ask for a hefty bribe if found not wearing one's seat belts. A recent study done by Maruti across 17 Indian cities showed that only 25% of car occupants used seat belts.

Moving on, let's talk more about driving experiences in India. I strongly believe that anyone who can drive here in India can certainly participate in X games. While driving in India – you need the eyesight of a hawk and attention level of God. From any nook and corn, a pedestrian can come at you running, or just a car in front of you think that it is a good idea to halt traffic in a single lane, just so he can take a U-turn. Let's talk about cows – the angels of the roads – the ones that shouldn't be disturbed while they cozy up on the roads and create a traffic jam for kilometers. One thing that completely behooves me is why on earth a dairy farmer would let loose his cows that end up in the middle of highways disrupting traffic? Cows are not the most intelligent creatures, if you blow the horn at a dog that is on the road, he will instantly react to it and would steer away from your way but for cows it is not the case. The added belief of cow being holier than thou makes us wait for this lazy animal to slowly move away from the road. I was browsing through the net the other day and found a video where a man from Spain filmed a cow that had somehow entered his backyard and this fascinated him greatly. As I read the comments on the post, many foreigners shared their stories how they once saw a cow on a road or a field and this was rare and unique to them while for me, an Indian, seeing cows everywhere isn't a surprise. If I go out of the house and don't see cows for about five minutes on the road, I would be surprised. I always wonder how we have made peace with the fact that if a herd of cows is in the middle of the road then we wouldn't be flabbergasted and would question our administration to take some severe steps not to allow the farmers to be irresponsible and allow these cows to go about create a havoc on the roads. To be honest, cows are one of the most innocent animals out there and it is the sole responsibility of their caretaker to take some god damn responsibility and not leave them to go wherever they please. The religious politics over cow and government policies have made the situation even worse. It is a dangerous situation for the animal as well as the humans.

Now, I like to believe that I have quite a good control over my anger; I don't get triggered easily and I have a good amount of patience in situations that can easily provoke a person with a little bit of temper. To test my patience level and anger comes in the Indian road sense. When you are driving your car, and on the road, you witness tractor with manure on its back, a heavy-duty truck on narrow lanes, buses trying to overtake you and an animal farm on the road — temper goes for a rollicking ride. I am honest with you, I have seen so much randomness on Indian roads; I have seen animals like cows, dogs, cats, horses, donkeys and monkeys appear out of nowhere on the Indian roads effectively halting moving traffic and creating chaos; I have seen people doing all kinds of things on the roads — people walking casually in the middle of the roads, people stopping without giving a moment's notice and creating a death scare, people jumping on the roads (while there is an overpass already built that is meant for the pedestrians to cross the road) and appearing before high-speed vehicles and I have seen people being caught up in ugly forms of accidents as well. It's not just the people walking on the roads but also the ones who are behind the wheels. First of all, traffic lights work when there are cops around (so people follow these lights due to fear of the cops); drivers don't really care about the convenience of other drivers on the road : Exhibit A, they can stop their car in the middle of the road to wait for someone, Exhibit B, they can take a U- turn out of nowhere because they have missed their turn, Exhibit C, they would honk at you mercilessly if you try to be a good citizen and stop at a red light when there is no visible traffic ahead. All these exhibits have been performed by everyone in this country. It's chaos out there; it's so bad to drive in India that every time you go out there it's like going on a rollercoaster ride with a faulty seatbelt.

This kind of chaotic traffic situation is the result of bad policing, lack of government interest in educating the masses about traffic safety and overall there is no real testing of driver's skill while he/she is getting a license. It's quite safe to say in India — to obtain a driving licence— you need to be above 18 and that's all. There is no driving test or any form of written test to see you actually know how to drive a two or a four-wheeler. Technically, I guess there is a written test (that's just a formality); everyone knows that no one can survive in an Indian road, if you learn about every small traffic rules and instructions. The network of roads in India is a jungle, and it's all about survival of the fittest — throw all the wisdom of safe driving outside and be the denizen of the chaos.

Yes, there are many solutions for this horrible traffic situation in India but no one is interested in them. I can't really understand that why this isn't brought into national consciousness. Politicians ask for votes by promising the building of new roads, but why don't we really focus on the traffic law and order on these roads? We boast that we are building new highways, overpasses, underpasses, tunnels etc yet we don't really see the bad state of traffic law and order. Why can't we as a country just say what we feel? I am undoubtedly confident that every single Indian knows about our traffic and road situation, yet it feels like roads will develop, people will upgrade to more savvy cars, but the dangerous chaos of the roads will be here, and no one will care for it to change.

Another thing that really plagues India are the conditions of the roads and it largely comes under the makeshift infrastructure of this country. I live in Noida, so I get to enjoy driving on one of the best roads India has to offer. Metropolitans and major cities of the country still have some good and drivable roads; while the rest of India have roads that can't be proudly pronounced as roads by any civil engineer. Even the major cities of the country have really sophisticated roads only near the airports or the VIP areas, while smaller pockets and old regions have the same substandard roads. Rural areas have dirt tracks or a patch of concrete that has disintegrated into potholes of numerous quantities. Small towns have tightly squeezed roads that remain congested throughout the day; there are either makeshift roads made of pebbles and dirt which are laid out in some areas or are very shoddily made government funded roads. Indian roads are made up of low-quality materials and are in constant need of repair, that it gets very rarely; and when it gets the due repair, it severely halts the traffic system with no systematic approach of construction activity. Indian politicians either orders to lay a brand-new road — when elections are near or give a counter-example of Indian roads with mentioning of few good roads laid near the rich areas of the city/village/town.

According to me, you can see the most insane amount of Indianness of India on the roads. You may ask why? If you are asking this, then you clearly haven't spent that much time in India. Indian roads are beautiful chaos — home to insane drivers and roadside vendors. The roads in India attract everything — from wildlife to human life — every chaotic activity is initiated from here. Roads are infamous for the beggars — small children selling toys, roses etc; breastfeeding women begging for money to feed her infant child; handicapped men and women asking for some change. The roads are a sight of misery as well as business. The business side of the roads comprises of hawkers and vendors. If you stop at a red light — there are chances of choreographed begging extravaganza or people trying to sell a variety of items — from pirated books to phone chargers — this overwhelming experience takes place in that minute's wait at the traffic signal.

You could find traffic in India for many reasons. Cows have overrun the roads to weird celebrations by people for various things — the most common is the *baraat*. Baraat is basically when Indians decide to make roads their discotheque and disrupt traffic for hours. The groom's family and friends in a giant moving discotheque covers a sizeable distance to the wedding venue— where the bride's family and friends await to welcome them. According to Indian astrology department, there are some golden months in a year when marriages are considered auspicious and in those months, people turn Indian roads into private discotheques. People in India just don't show their excitement during marriage season but on several occasions — various festivals or when Indian wins an important cricket match or some politician's hullabaloo. People in India just need a reason to head to their favourite party destination — the Indian roads.

Now, Indian roads are where the Indian gastronomy lies; if Paris is all about its street side cafes, then India is all about random shops at every corner of the roads. People eat at the roads and paint it with the leftovers. Dustbins are either ignored or are missing — so the roads have to take the mess of whatever people eat and throw. Roads are the favourite parking spot for morons; roads are the unofficial bus and auto stops; roads are the favourite walking ground for stray dogs; roads are the perfect spittoons for tobacco eaters. Roads are the most used public space in India and it is where the most Indianness can be seen. From the chaotic traffic to the celebration of all kind; from jaywalkers to the unofficial hawker's paradise — Indian roads is where the party's at. I think if Buddha was alive today, he would reconsider his Zen attitude while driving on an Indian road.

I can give you many solutions — but they all feel vague now — impose fines and get more advertisements telling about road safety — they are all being done but without any sizeable effect. I believe what we can do is to educate the younger generations thoroughly. We have English, Hindi or one native language, Social Science, Science and Maths as compulsory subjects in schools; now just make a small addition of another subject namely Civic Sense which would also include a Chapter on Traffic safety and Instructions. This concept would work in two ways — firstly it will educate the small children and their parents and teachers who are forced to read them to teach the children. In India, if it boils down to scoring good marks, parents would take it seriously and thus a cycle of conditioning of children would result in a new generation of well-informed citizens and this might even create an impression on parents; and yes, make this subject as important as above-mentioned subjects.

How can we inculcate civic sense?

Now let's push forward this model of discussion in pertaining to civic experiences. My solution here is to make civic sense as compulsory subjects in school across this nation (I am aware that in many schools we have moral science but that is something that is not taken seriously by students, teachers and even parents). If we make civic sense as important as teaching maths and science in schools, then we can start a process of churning out citizens who are educated in traditional as well as moral sense. In India, education is about scoring good marks in tests and exams — parents and teachers want good marks — students are scared into trying to score marks. Now, I want students to fight for marks in Civic Sense (on the record, I am totally against the horrible education system of India); at least in the cut throat competition of scoring marks, they will learn traffic rules, appropriate public behaviour and many other things that we are going to discuss further; as I mentioned earlier, this will create a cycle, parents and teacher would have to read their child's textbook in order to teach them—thus knowingly educating their children and unknowingly educating themselves in civic sense. We, Indians get a basic schooling education, and then we get a college education, yet we remain quite uneducated in terms of civic sense. Why is that? Does it mean that education in India is just limited to helping children go to college and then learn to earn money via jobs? Why aren't we concerned about their morality and good citizen behaviour? In schools, we don't forget to make our kids learn about our rich history, our freedom struggles, our national icons and about the length and breadth of our country, but sadly we forget to teach them how to be a good citizen of this nation. The schools are affected by the political nature of the society, which is all about being a passive singer of praise for this nation. Schools

14

are more concerned in telling India is great but not discussing how can we make it a better place for us to live in. We are not addressing any problem in the classrooms, or frankly speaking anywhere but just skirting around the problems. Why shall we restrict this to the classrooms, we should have this subject in the curriculum of higher education— in colleges and universities as well. I like to believe that people of all age groups in India are quite lacking in the subject of civic sense; there is no shame in learning about them. We should look at those developed countries where people have been pioneers in civic sense— their social structure and how they are so efficient should be our role model.

Not in my Backyard

There is a very famous saying, "Not in my backyard". This phrase which in its acronym form is known as NIMBY is used by local communities resisting any form of hazardous activity that is being carried out by a corporation or the government. Though in India, we may not use this term often or to some extent don't use this phrase, but we certainly adhere to it.

For us, the Indians, it's quite all right to be ignorant about anything that is outside our own backyards. Our country has a serious cleanliness problem. The roads outside our houses have become a safe haven for all form of domestic garbage. Sidewalks are painted with the stains of tobacco splatters and animal excreta. If there is an empty plot or land, it automatically becomes a dumping ground. This dumping ground then attracts street dogs and grazing cows; in no time mosquitoes also gets this invitation to join the party.

Basically, outside our backyard, we are surrounded by unattended garbage. Parents scold their children when they throw any snack wrapper in their own houses or cars; and rightly so, but this teaching or scolding is only limited to their own properties. If you are eating something in your car, it's a sin in the eyes of many Indians to litter in their own cars because roads are right there to be made a garbage dump. If you have been to India — you would certainly observe the callous attitude of throwing stuff or spitting from moving cars out there on the roads. The reason here is NIMBY or even out of my sight out of my mind.

Public properties like parks, beaches, roads, monuments etc have fallen victim to this beautiful attitude. This NIMBY attitude is quite common in every class throughout this country.

Rich people would want to live in clean house and surroundings and poor people only have the option of one—just the clean house. People would never think of drawing graffitis or vandalising the walls of their own houses, but the same people would have no qualms in thrashing the walls of historical sites, public properties, monuments etc.

It's not that dustbins are not placed but they are blink and miss type of structures. In some places, there are proper disposal facilities but may lack in collection and maintenance methodology; but in overwhelming majority these dustbins are either missing or overflown in capacity. People in this country are familiar with the concept of dustbins but it's limited to their house or when they visit a fancy restaurant or a mall. I would say the government is sleeping in this whole waste disposal fiasco and the public are too ignorant to care about it. This problem of garbage everywhere in this country is not a new problem but one that has largely remained unattended for years. The government makes promises, people eat it up. The people teach their children not to litter in their own properties but are the first ones to tell them to throw their garbages out there in the streets. This needs strict action, and if this problem doesn't come in priority list or gains the numero uno situation, then what does? An Indian has learnt to close his/her nose when encountering a garbage heap, dodge the buffet of animal excreta and other forms of garbage but haven't learnt that this shouldn't be the state of affairs.

People who visit from other countries never really able to figure out why we live in such dirty conditions; to them, I would like to say, it's a mystery that even we are not able to solve. Clearly the country we look up to is all spick and span. When Indians get a chance to visit a developed country, the first thing they notice is the cleanliness all around. They see dustbins everywhere — used by the public and maintained by the government. We come home, we tell our relatives and friends about this lovely phenomenon of not seeing garbage everywhere— the friends and family who haven't visited abroad would listen to these experiences with a sparkle in their eyes. This longing and dream how it's like to be part of a society that clearly has social etiquettes and have learnt how to throw garbage in a dustbin boggles Indian minds. Indians abroad throw garbage where it is supposed to go, but back home where there is no repercussion, they automatically switch to their earlier mentality of creating a mess; it clearly shows that we like to live in a society which is clean. We clearly see a problem here, yet we fail to address it. It's an Indian problem and unless we figure out how to move past it, we will always feel inferior to other nations.

This cleanliness problem is a civic sense issue; one that I propose should be a chapter in the suggested compulsory subject of 'Civic Sense'. I won't show naivety here by saying, that oh let us impose strict fines on people throwing garbage here and there. Brilliant idea, implemented by many nations but this idea comes around and never goes around in India. Everyone suggests that let the cops impose fines on people throwing garbage. I won't suggest this, and you ask why? It won't be a success because like the popular opinion of littering all around, cops too have this habit embedded in them and just like any other Indian, they too have a habit of littering. How can they take this fine scheme seriously, if they are also the part of the problem? Plus, police corruption and misuse of power is already a big concern in India — that implementing any such scheme would breed more corruption and misuse of police power. The only solution here is a nationwide education (not the kind that is just to entice people temporarily to get votes). I have suggested my 'Civic Sense solution' and there are many brilliant Indian minds who have ideas or even are implementing in their own personal capacity to address this issue; but when you want to change more than a billion souls, you need national-level leaders and faces to acknowledge this seriously and put forward solutions to address this problem, till then we live in this mess like we had been living for so many years.

The Toilet Conundrum

In India — public urination is prevalent to rural as well as urban spheres and open defecation is a problem more relevant and centric to rural areas — there might be toilets constructed in accordance to some government scheme but still somehow choosing to defecate outdoors takes precedent. People make the roads and the open areas their own toilets. Urinating on the side of the streets is one of the most common sights in India — from swanky metropolis to the most disjointed rural area — you would find some gentlemen showering the walls. What is the problem here? Why do people feel the need to urinate, defecate and spit outside? Is it some kind of weird Indian fetish? No, again it all boils down to lack of civic sense and education.

It all circles down to one thing – first, lack of education and then its subset, that is civic sense. Finding civic sense in India is an effort equivalent to locating lost ships and planes in the Bermuda Triangle. People in India, both educated and the uneducated have one thing in common, lack of civic sense. This lack of civic sense reflects when you step outside in the streets of our country — the chaos of the traffic — people throwing random garbage at random places — people spitting, peeing and doing unspeakable things out in the open. Lack of civic sense is the direct result of a population that is gigantic — and when there are these many people — resources are shared to such an extent that even performing basic tasks in this country becomes an uphill battle. Now let's not digress and talk about our fascination with peeing outside and doing other functions that should be reserved for the bathrooms. The government in this country is inept — the demands of maintaining the toilets owned and operated by the government — the infamous 'Sulabh Sauchalaya' are the worst kind of toilets that you can come across. The toilets are so bad and mismanaged that relieving yourself out on the roads is a better and a more hygienic option. But the blame is not entirely on the authorities but the brilliant people of this country — who can destroy public property in a matter of minutes.

Let's talk about the rural areas — where television and smartphones have become a common commodity, yet toilets have not broken through common usage spheres. For Indian men — they have the audacity to go about their business in the open forested areas at any time of the day — while the women don't enjoy such a luxury. Now, the women cannot go in the night or even in the day, because of their safety concerns — many times, sexual predators or voyeurs would wait for women to come out in the woods. It's called nature's call but for women in the rural areas, they must go early in the morning to relieve themselves; the thing in India is that if it isn't affecting the men, then it isn't really a problem. Toilets are not a matter of concern for some rural areas, they have adjusted to life like this — giving excuses like 'toilets cannot be near the house where there is holy temple and the kitchen where food is cooked'. The attitude where the toilet is not a priority has effectively made the rural areas in India feel like an archaic society when compared to rest of the world. If even in the technological age of 2017, toilets are deemed unnecessary, then something fundamentally wrong is happening. I am not even going to point out to the health risk of open defecation but rather want to first draw comparison that if you live in a civilised community, then this practice of doing your business outside pushes the term civilised community in contrast to the rural tribes who are oblivious of technological advancements and that of animals who don't have the intellectual prowess of knowing where to urinate and defecate.

As for the people urinating out on the roads in India needs to be publicly embarrassed. In India the only tool that works is the fear of Gods and some property owners have put up the picture of Gods and Goddesses in the hopes of people being respectful enough not to urinate on the walls that have the faces of the Gods. This is so ironic — how the gods must be used to educate fully grown adults not to pee on every wall of the country — frankly it's embarrassing and it gives rise to the question: when shall we start addressing the chaotic civic sense problem that had and has been haunting our country for years and will haunt for several years to come?

Are we ignorant of racism in India?

In India racism is a big problem and what is harrowing is the lack of awareness regarding this. You google — most racist countries in the world and India ranks among the top contenders. In India racism happens on counts like the colour of your skin, facial features and caste you belong to.

Dark skinned Indians hailing from the south of India and even other parts of the country faces a casual form of racism; Africans who are either students or working in India face racism of more vivid and destructive form; Dalits and anyone of lower castes or untouchables had and has been facing discrimination, segregation and racism. Casual fun is also racism. When condescendingly called '*chinki*' or 'chinese' in their own country, people from North East India feel threatened and dejected from Indian identity. North Eastern women are stereotyped so heavily — and often become easy targets of sexual harassment. The insinuation of a northeastern woman of being a prostitute or massage therapist is grossly offensive and racist. Northeastern men are either stereotyped as security guards and by being called as Nepalis. They are heavily stereotyped and are always judged that they are up to no good. Similarly, people coming from African countries feels racism at every level. People always assume that they are up to no good. The hypocrisy lies in the fact that if Indians are smoking and playing loud music — no one bats an eye but when an African does that — it gives the mob an intention of being violent. The deep-rooted hatred for Africans and Northeastern can be visibly seen. They are not easily given living spaces by tenants. They are often harassed by the public and as well as the police. Based on the colour of their skin and facial features, they get harassed, stereotyped and discriminated. Now in the opposite of such experiences, Indians worship white skin foreigners. I don't understand if its colonial hangover or what — Indians feel that a white skinned person is superior. Indian obsession with white skin can be seen from the fact that white skin is promoted in every sphere. We get to see fairness cream advertisement constantly. We made a society where fair skin is a mark of superiority. Actors and actresses who are fair are more likely to catch the public eye. Similarly, Indians are obsessed with fair skinned foreigners. These foreigners as opposed to African nationals or even East Asian nationals doesn't face racism of such sort. People get so fascinated by naive curiosity, that they stop them and click pictures with them — alleviating them to a pedestal because of their fair skin.

Now, let's talk about racism in a more domestic sense. South Indian states and many other states have indigenous dark-skinned men and women. They might not face racism in a direct way but our popular culture has been staged in such a way that fair skin is worshipped. People in North India with lighter skin tone casually make fun of dark skinned Indian nationals; mainstream television stereotypes various Indian nationalities; popular comedian normalizes racism by making them seen as harmless jokes. Racism in India is also quite sexist in nature. If a man is dark skinned but has a decent job will be qualified to seek a bride with a fair skin tone. Look at the matrimonial ads — it's all about asking for fair skin brides. Girls with dark skin are often made fun of and considered as a burden on parents. Dark skin is synonymous in India with ugliness and unattractiveness; to be honest, anyone seeing colour to judge beauty is ugly to the core. Mainstream movies have racist jokes and songs; we, as an ignorant country enjoys them. The ones who don't face racism says that there is no racism and the ones who face racism finds themselves helpless to even make people look at their problem seriously. In a country where poverty, hunger and basic facilities haunts people, racism is put on the back burner and isn't considered a serious offense.

23

India is a very complicated country – and the racism doesn't just end simply with skin colour – it boils down to your caste and creed. The caste system is complicated and a racist system to begin with. The caste system has effectively divided the system and has seeped so deeply in our Indian society – that it has become a barometer of social interactions. So, if you are of a caste that is of higher order, say a Brahmin or a Rajput, it is a sin for you to even interact with a person of lower caste say a Dalit or Shudra. This divide that was made centuries ago to suppress certain class purely out of political ambitions is still relevant in the modern age. In India, marriages only happen between the members of the same caste or castes of same social standings. If in any exception, a marriage between a higher caste and a lower caste is heard of – it becomes a social taboo or the worst-case scenario is the route of mob lynching or the dreadful honour killing. Racism done via caste hierarchy is quite prevalent in our country — Dalits and untouchables are denied access to public places and temples. They are ostracised from villages and are made to conduct professions suited to their castes. Racism is so deeply based on castes, that a person of higher caste even in this modern day and age would hesitate to sit and eat with a person of lower caste. Lower caste minorities often face police brutality and denial of basic fundamental rights. Dalits and lower caste population have been facing racism of various forms and the societal structure is so skewed that it has been normalised over time.

Why foreign tourists find their Indian experience as bittersweet?

India is a country that has its own unique voice; such a voice attracts an influx of tourists who want to travel the exotic tropical land. The century-old monuments and temples and a strong historical significance creates a spectacle that captivates the minds of people around the world. The country has so much to offer: food that has its own standing; culture so unique that it can't be replicated; historical significance of paramount importance and yet there's a weird sense of hitch that foreign tourists experience before visiting India.

Most travellers from the western countries, who clearly are different in every aspect to the denizens of our country, often gets surprised from the fact that how the vast majority of Indians gets taken aback when they encounter them. Tourists with pale white skin or even chocolate black skin find themselves as an object of amazement. As we earlier mentioned, our country is mostly a population of less educated or uneducated men and women; there isn't a great exchange in terms of intercountry communication and there is a dearth of social etiquettes that persists. The simple-minded people of this country get fascinated by these first world dwellers who in their eyes seems altogether a whole different species — their skin and hair colour is all different from the tropical features of brown and black respectively; the way of dressing is different. All these factors make them an object of amazement in the eyes of these common Indian folks. It's harmless to be fascinated by people from different countries but this harmlessness is meted by Indians in a bizarre way that tells about our lack of social etiquettes.

This weird Indian habit of staring makes people very uncomfortable. The majority population that is socially uneducated in the subject of civic sense and social etiquettes makes the tourists from another country (that have a strong social and cordial environment) queasy and feel out of place. As a citizen of this country, I know the curiosity that many of the Indians have — due to their economic constraints, they are unlikely to visit another country and encounter people of different kinds. But on the other hand, it makes me embarrassed when foreign tourists assess that every staring Indian is the image of every Indian living.

Now, this fascination is two-faceted: harmless and harmful. It's harmless when people get fascinated and tries to interact with foreign tourists constructively. There are wonderful Indians who aide these tourists by providing them shelter, assistance and food. This is a positive exchange. But sadly, this experience gets overshadowed by the harmful fascination. People staring foreign tourists make them grossly uncomfortable; the foremost complaint by foreign women travelling in India is that everyone is staring them continuously and sometimes it borders into perversion. Though, it's pathetic to defend such a complaint, because even the Indian women face these pervert stares almost every day. Now, whenever a foreign tourist accuses our country of allegations (that are almost all correct), we go into a frenzy and finds ourselves in a defensive mode. We somehow point our fingers to these foreign tourists of not dressing up appropriately or being too westernised for their own good. Holy shit, we are defending cases of sexual harassment and assault. It's bad that we have a severe women safety issue already in this country but also have this habit of defending the aggressor. There have been so many cases of sexual misconduct towards women who travels to India, that many countries have put out warnings on their official sites and provided a list of do's and don'ts for their citizens while visiting India. If this doesn't break your jingoism and this feeling that Indian culture is the best, then you, sir, are the part of a problem. A very few people

26

are willing to address this problem. As one of the millions of educated diasporas who wants tourists from other countries to feel safe here in India, it feels embarrassing when these people go back to their country with good memories outweighed by bad ones. Due to the conduct of few rotten people, the whole country's name gets spoilt. People should realize that even the action of a single individual can cast an impression of a whole country. If you really want to show patriotism — then instead of dancing on the streets clad in the colours of your favourite political party and yelling chants of jingoism, be respectful and be helpful to anyone visiting our country.

We have a racism problem in our country that no one is aware of. Again, the excuse will be the simple-minded uneducated folks. I believe to become better citizens of this country, we need to shed this defense mechanism that we automatically develop whenever someone points a finger at our country. We, as a country still recovering from colonial hangover feels anyone with white skin is automatically superior and anyone with dark skin is inferior. Look at our advertisements, where cosmetics are aimed at showing how you can whiten your dark skin; television and mainstream films showcasing this ever so casually how fair-skinned people are more beautiful and successful. Foreign tourists who have white skin find themselves surrounded and hailed as some sort of superior beings. They are stopped randomly and coerced into taking selfies with people around them. Why do Indians want to take selfie with a random tourist? It all boils down to the white skin which signifies to the Indians some sort of superiority. Everywhere, these fair skinned tourists either get countless demands for selfies or face awkward encounters. They are here to travel at their own leisure and just like any human being enjoys their privacy. These foreign tourists feel so weird that how the colour of their skin which doesn't really amount much in their home country makes them superior in India. On the other hand, tourists who have

27

black skin (African descent) are subjected to the opposite behaviour received by their fair-skinned counterparts. They are being harassed, bullied and often called names. This behaviour is due to their black skin and different appearance, which in Indian notebook of race hierarchy is quite low. Our country is so deep dwelled into racism, that we have learnt to ignore them effectively. There have been many cases of mob violence against black tourists across India. In a nutshell we find ourselves attracted to fair skin while despising black skin people — and that's textbook racism. Again, the defense would be simple-minded uneducated Indian folks. Well, the racism problem cuts quite deep and the most surprising fact is that we as a country are quite ignorant about it.

The problem here is that we don't have the civic attitude to respect the privacy of others; as a country we have somehow accepted it but people visiting us have a hard time digesting the fact that as a country we lack tremendously in social etiquettes and have no civic obligation towards each other. The next time you throw any waste outside ever so casually or urinate at the side of a road or just be ignorant as possible; remember that this is a lifelong impression you are giving to ones who are visiting our country.

Though India has a lot to offer in terms of historical monuments and cultural experiences, somehow, we come across as a nation of congestion and bad manners. People directly engaged in tourism economy comes across in a bad light; from taxi drivers to tourist guides — either they mistreat tourists or try to overcharge them or straight out harass them. Overwhelmingly, they don't realize in a way they are representing their country. To say that India is the best or support a politician isn't a litmus test of your national pride but rather how you treat your own citizen as well citizens from other countries. Foreign tourists will only carry the memory of their one on one experiences with Indian locals; it's sad to say that majority of these interactions turns out to be unpleasant. Sometimes it feels, we are fortunate to have acumen like Taj Mahal that is able to attract foreign tourists because if it had been left to the government and public initiative to make India, a tourist-friendly country, we would have had failed miserably.

The Indian Language Conundrum

A country like ours is unique and spectacular in the sense that it houses a wide plethora of languages. According to the census of 2001, there are 1635 rationalised mother tongues, 234 identifiable mother tongues and 22 major languages. Of these, 29 languages have more than a million native speakers, 60 have more than 100,000 and 122 have more than 10,000 native speakers. This is insane. This is utterly beautiful. This is chaotic. This is confusing. This is India. The country had and has been living with people in every direction speaking different languages or either speaking different dialects, variations and accents of the particular languages. Move in any direction, from north to south or east to west; you would encounter different cultures, customs, traditions and languages. This is the heart of diversity in India.

As we all know, Hindi is the language that majority of the population in this country speaks and which amounts to roughly half the population; now the other half speaks Bengali, Tamil, Telugu, Marathi, Gujarati, Oriya, Malayalam, Urdu, Kannada and many other. The country has such a large population that even the half that doesn't really converses in the language of the majority amounts to a number that can fill up multiple countries (if you compare these populations to the western countries). Now, the country to bridge the communication gap try to inculcate Hindi into the national conscience. People all around the country (second language speakers) make a good chunk who can understand and speak Hindi (though not with the perfect finesse of the native Hindi speakers). But it is ignorant for people who majorly speak Hindi to assume and expect everyone in India to be proficient in Hindi; only the educated percentage gets exposure to Hindi in schools and colleges.

The uneducated population and in India it is humongous and are only limited to their own native languages (they are not even well versed to write or read their native languages); and I cannot emphasise enough that India has such a huge population that when you say minority, it also makes a huge portion of the population.

Now, this language gap, where the ignorants on both sides — Hindi and non-Hindi speakers clash. Politicians like the opportunists that they are, try to win over the population with the sentiment that their native language is superior. For example, if the central government is mostly North centric, then they would put forward policies that is more favourable to a Hindi speaker or the states in north who are more or less have learned to accept Hindi as their second language; but the states down South or in the East that have just accepted the idea of Hindi as a language that is a secondary option and not very compulsory in nature; politicians down south would enforce the idea that their particular native language is either superior or is being oppressed by Hindi. This weird sentiment that their language and cultural identity is at risk has created an age-old North-South divide. The educated and intelligent on both sides, welcome each other but the uneducated and the opportunistic politicians try to create a rift. Funnily, the divide is not prominently seen in North or East or West or even Central India, which too have a language gap, but more visible in North and South. In this equation, a third language sweeps in massaging the egos of both language conservatives on both sides. The International lingua franca — English is proving to be a language that is in fact making interactions amongst North and South alive. The superior attitude of the North and the reluctant attitude of South to accept Hindi wholly have paved the way for mature and intelligent people on both sides who consider states in North and South as a part of their own country and have accepted English as a good way for communication.

Languages in India are a tricky business; but the divide between North and South casts a sentiment sometimes that they are different countries that are merged into one. I can't really explain it, but due to some miracle, we still have this collective national feeling of India still intact. I get it, people in both the directions have doubts and fingers pointing at each other; they have different skin colours, languages, customs, upbringings, mannerisms, mindsets and frankly a majority of things yet the history of collective freedom from the colonial power unites the nation. Frankly in modern times pop culture which has thrust actors, singers, scientists and national leaders as flag bearers of the country which has made people down south and up north see and relate to their fellow countrymen. I believe the language war would only cease, if we stop imposing Hindi down south, and the south starts relaxing about the annexation of their individual identity and start to accept Hindi as a second language that they can put their efforts to learn (just to connect with their fellow countrymen). I am suggesting the importance of English for chiefly Hindi speakers (because they can't be expected to learn one of the many native languages in the country). Now, the whole language problem's solution lies in the education of the masses. If we have more people educated, we'll have a greater section of people in North speaking English, and down south we would have more Hindi as well as English speakers. Politicians rather fighting over language struggle and inciting hatred amongst people should rather just focus on education, slowly but surely language struggle would seem to ease down.

What instigates communal riots?

I am going to start this topic of communal riots with the motherload — Partition of India and Pakistan — that showcased how brutal, we humans can be. Communities that lived in peace were shredded to pieces — Hindus, Sikhs and Muslims — all suffered. Women were raped and killed; children were slaughtered mercilessly; men killed men all in the name of their religion and community. Now, since that horrific experience, India started on a path where we somehow accepted the idea of diversity. People from different religions learnt to live together and had been living in the same neighbourhoods; tolerant of each other's houses of worship; respectable of each other's festivals and celebrations. But somehow from that experience of blood from the time of the infamous Partition, we did experience many major and as well as minor communal riots in India.

We, Indians had this big debate a few years ago, the infamous tolerance vs intolerance; here you heard loud jingoism, ignorance and botched up biases. Let's throw some facts here. Out of 198 countries that were analysed by the Pew Research Centre, India ranked the fourth worst in the world for religious intolerance. To deny this is stupid. To be defensive of this is ignorant. To be proud of this — is messed up. People often argue tolerance by giving examples of countries that are grossly intolerant — like Majority Muslim countries that suppress minorities and are notorious in their human rights exercises. Firstly, no one is saying that what those countries are doing the right thing; every country that boasts itself as a flag bearer of progress and peace condemns such state of affair and obviously doesn't want to adopt such behaviour. Our country with a majority Hindu population doesn't need to be competing with infamous Muslim majority countries notorious for human rights, minority rights and women's rights violations. In a nutshell, we want to be a better place and that should be the foremost aspiration, not that we are at least better than some regressive countries. We are India, a land where Hindus, Muslims, Sikhs and Isaias had and have been living together with an identity that speaks in unison of Indian brotherhood. To be saying that to be secular is more or less pro-Muslim, then you are part of a sick propaganda and belief system that has been effectively boiling the Hindu-Muslim tensions. I have to spell this out — if Hindu killing Muslims is evil, so is the other way round. No one is encouraging the extremist interpretation of Islam, let the law decide if either a Muslim or a Hindu whoever harms in any way receives his/her due punishment.

Due to weird propagandas throughout India, hatred has been put in the opposing communities, namely Hindus and Muslims. The hatred for Muslims is due to the sour taste of Mughal rule in the past which saw some intolerant regimes and rulers. The terrorist implications and strongholds of our neighbouring country have also left a sour taste. Now, all this has made a generalisation problem. It's obvious that terrorism in no way should be endorsed; it's obvious that any act of hatred in the name of Islam shouldn't be ignored; but why do we view Muslims who have nothing to do with extremist propaganda to appear as victims in a circle of generalisation. The Muslims that are killed in such riots are mostly the innocent commoners; the ones instigating them (either a Hindu or a Muslim) are benefitting politically. Hindus have somehow adopted a deep-rooted hatred for Islam, and Islam with the religion of extreme devotion has made its followers in a defensive army of beliefs that they would fight tooth and nail to protect their doctrines. Hindus dislike Muslims because of the majority always has this lingering belief of some sort of birth right because of numerical advantage; Muslims because of their stubborn belief system also want their minority to hold up to be of opposing view and ready to counter Hindu hostility with hostility.

Now, here we have two religious groups, living in a country that is prone to riots at any escalation. From the hypothetical dangers of Muslim uprising (civil war scenario) to the dangers of Hindu uprising (ethnic cleansing), we still somehow managed to find ourselves in the central safe zone. Though we have communal tensions and riots here and there, still we have been successful enough that we didn't have any form of civil war and ethnic cleansing scenario, despite our neighbouring countries have and had been the experience holders of both. This clearly means that setting aside the jingoistic Hindus and the extremist Muslims, all of us wants peace. Despite many citizens having a feeling of doubt and objections of each other's religions, we somehow want a society that remains stable and a country that has stable governance. If the majority is not the part of hate that can bring about civil war, then what brings out the communal riots here and there?

The answer is the politicians, who pull the strings of hatred according to their convenience and escalates tensions between Hindus and Muslims. No one has the time, energy and hatred deep enough to go on and spread communal hatred; the common people of this country, want a nation that treats them fairly and justly; they have and had been fine with neighbours with different religions than theirs; the country celebrates many religious festivals, where neighbours of different religions greet each other and enjoy each other's company. The riots, hate speeches and talks of 'Saffron State' and 'Islamic State' are made by people who see profit in different polarising communities. Hindu leaders create hysteria, by pointing out isolated incidences of killing, looting and raping, portraying all Muslims as evil; their counterparts creates hysteria by playing minority card, putting Kashmir in the mix and their isolates incidences of killing, looting and raping. Again, any form of crime (regardless of its perpetrators being of any religion) falls in the purview of the judiciary; don't mock the victims and the affected by referring isolated incidents in the mix pumping mass hysteria, fear and hatred for each other. For religious vote banks, politicians are ready to divide a Hindu-Muslim mix; they don't care about the houses burnt, people killed and injured; they only see the votes, and divide the people who never had this hate, but now have found a reason for hatred provided via a carefully constructed narrative by various politicians.

It's human folly to be of critical in nature; our mind has this survival instinct — always telling us about the upcoming dangers. The excitable humans find it easy to know their enemy — so a person with a belief system different to theirs can be seen as a potential danger. Now, this suspicion is played out, and the majority of masses (with same belief system) starts to see minority with different belief systems as someone they need to be wary of. Any form of indiscretion from a few in this minority population by doing anything stupid will give the majority or maybe confirming their fears about these 'people' who are a danger to them and their families. This hysteria gets played by the ones in power, spread through media in propaganda and thus we can see the culmination of hatred formed out of pure speculation and psychological fears.

I am out of depth here in providing a solution; I have seen enough images of horror of different religions clashing with each other; this is humanity at peril. Our country has seen many horrors, where Hindus are killing Muslims (infamous Godhra riots) in retaliation for Muslims killing Hindu passengers in a train. Muslims extremism is retaliating in forms of terrorist attacks, namely 26/11 attacks on Mumbai. If I go on, there would be a huge list of communal riots between not only Hindu and Muslim but other religions in India as well. We also saw the Sikh massacre in 1984. We have seen enough horrors as a country where people of India suffered. There are numerous acts of radical Islamic terrorism that haunted us. There are acts of violence in every spectrum yet we as a country are standing firm. Maybe some question our diversity and secular viewpoints, but this is what has made India free from any form of civil war and ethnic cleansing scenarios. The country is not that weak that it would kneel down to a faction of religious fanatics, carrying out acts of hatred and violence. This proves that if we actually learn about people and not judge them by their religion, we can end any force-fed hatred from the ones in power; for a while and maybe in a state of epiphany, we will see the love for the neighbours of different faiths.

Sports and India

In India there is religion, then there are almost religions like Cricket. The sport has such a massive following in India, that it overshadows every other sport in such a heavy margin, that tips the scale so much in Cricket's favour that as a country we have been neglecting other sports.

It's lovely to see Cricket being so big in India; cricketers are idols and some like Sachin Tendulkar who has been devotedly termed as the 'God of Cricket'. Why can't we have even a fraction of love in hearts reserved for other sports and their players? The country has undoubtedly one of the best teams in the world of Cricket; we have won laurels that made the country collectively proud; we recall stories of Cricket matches that made us cry out of sheer joy; we idolise cricketers and make them superstars.

Now, when you look at other sports — there is sheer neglect on every part. Government sports organisation doesn't take them as seriously as they take Cricket as a sport, there is little encouragement by parents and society towards young children trying out their hands at a non-Cricket sport and then there's the lack of audience or general mass disinterest in any sport that is not Cricket. This attitude of ours had made us suffer severely; the sports that are popular all over the world — where countries of half our size and quarter of our population are able to achieve international laurels. Despite being the second populous country, we never see our Olympics medal tally move past single digit whereas our neighbour China rakes up hundreds of medals. So, shall we assume, that more than a billion people living in this country are only interested in a single sport?

We have national interests as well as a pool of talent in sports (to name a few) like Badminton, Tennis, Football, Kabaddi, Hockey etc. These days we see the rise of sports icon in various sports. We see icons in many but, our attention spans are limited to some months after the glory. We do win international laurels time to time in various sports, but again the national memory forgets them quite quickly. As a nation, we remember every major trophy Indian Men's Cricket team has won but we would fail to list out major achievements in other sports. Now, when I say that India is ignorant of any sport that is not Cricket, then my criticism goes out to everyone and that includes me as well.

Lack of importance is given to sports in schools and colleges. Cricket is the only exception that teachers and parents take seriously; other sports suffer from their lack of proven success. Indians are quite rigid in future planning for their children; they see that the world demands engineers and doctors — so they would urge their children to become one. Now as for sports — they see a promising future only in Cricket in India, they would only let their children to be seriously coached in that game. Other sports suffer due to their weak credentials in India. Yes, there are exceptions, but they are in the minority. Only the upper middle or rich class can bear the risk of investing in their children who want to make a future that isn't in Cricket. This makes a minor portion of the population to be actively involved in playing, promoting and honing any other non-Cricket sport.

The country also suffers from a very weird belief that conventional education is superior to sporting education. For the older and more conservative generation or school of thoughts, sports is a mere distraction or method of staying physically fit and is not to be taken seriously at all. Studying and scoring marks in schools and colleges to get a good job is all that matters. We have a very famous Indian saying, '*Padhoge Likhoge banoge nawab, Kheloge kudoge toh hoge kharaab*'.

It means that 'if you study you shall become a respected individual, if you play you shall amount to nothing'. Parents have often used it to encourage their children to study and not waste time in playing.

As a nation, we have this rudimentary mindset that physical education is inferior to conventional forms of education. The country with a sizeable middle-class population wants their children to not take any form of risks and only see sports as a form of hobby or recreational activity. Talent is abundant in every sport but at the grassroots level — infrastructure and management are absent. The government does nothing concrete in promoting sports and trying to improve them. The sporting facilities in this country are abysmal and when we see national as well as international level sports person being treated poorly by the government sporting management, then the heart is lost in the hopes of improving the sporting situation in this country. When a career in sports is only viable for the rich who can afford private services, the abundance of talent and passion gets lost due to inept government management. It is hopeless to wonder that we will be able to achieve successes in Olympics and other International events comparatively to that of China or the US; the overwhelming difference in mindsets, infrastructure, facilities and the management —set us back to the bottom. The country has talent but the government and the society keep on failing its athletes and sportsperson time and time again; hypocrisy is shown by us, when some exceptional sportsperson win laurels; we start glorifying him/her, as if we really cared and the government would start rewarding the sportsperson and the media makes him/her a star. This is hypocrisy because the system was designed for him/her to fail but because of a stellar attitude — he/she won a laurel for the country. This is a slap on our faces that we are so ignorant of sports in India that we expect laurels in every competition but don't have the heart to help ailing sportsperson of this country.

Beggars of India: Theatrical tragedy?

Go to any part of the country — you will find some things in common — people breaking all the basic civic rules and beggars at every traffic signals. For us, the sight of beggars is so common that like the other problems in this country, we simply ignore them. Unemployment and lack of education have paved the way for the heavy number of beggars in the country; they live in below poverty line bracket surviving by the skin of their teeth. They are oblivious to any form of necessities like health, sanitation, housing, clothing etc. These people only struggle to get food twice a day (if they are lucky enough).. Due to the lack of education, the people in this below the poverty line have many children — who unfortunately from the day they open their eyes are thrust into begging on the streets.

In India — small children, women with a baby in their arms, old men and some with disabilities are the common sight in every traffic signal. Men and women who are fit works mostly as day labourers earning pennies; a vicious cycle forms and the only exposure a child born in a beggar's family will be rag picking, begging on the streets and sadly a life of crime. These small children mostly have tumultuous family relations, poor housing conditions and wear whatever they get in second-hand wear from middle class or rich people; in an escape, they would resort to taking drugs and even committing crimes.

It's such a weird sight to see cows moving freely on main roads and the encounters with women showcasing fragile little newborns to get some money from you; it's disheartening to see beggars have to resort to theatricals in order to get some money from people. It's a simple equation, if a man/woman/child who seems healthy and in a normal condition, you wouldn't

41

get sympathetic enough to shell out some money; while on the other hand if there is manipulation of emotions, then sympathy would overcome, and you would shell some money for the beggar. That's why we have so many handicapped beggars with arms and legs amputated asking for money; from blind beggars to mute ones, you can see the human theatrical that would move you to sympathy. You would see little children begging and crying for food; you would see mothers with newborn in hands crying; you would see endless misery and poverty yet the country sleeps in a belief that we rank amongst the top nations. These sights are horrible and should be eradicated; no politicians have its agenda set on this because their voting population doesn't care about this. The problem that beggars hadn't become a limited sight (that it should have been) is damning enough to see that years pass and politicians change, but poverty remains and the middle classes (who are the chief voters) doesn't give a damn.

Beggars have to resort to theatrics to seek our attention; syndicates who are running begging squads know this and they mercilessly make their subjects amputees, blind, dumb and what not. If this isn't the human tragedy of priority, then what is? What is the point of launching bullet trains or making exaggerated claims of India being developing, when we have human lives living in a perpetual hell? Eradication of poverty is the first step towards development and we Indians have been confused by the lies of our elected politicians. We are all engaged in pointless social media debates about what Hindus said about Muslims and vice-versa; we are so engrossed in our VIP culture and celebrity culture that no one sees the crux problems; we are so enthralled by the smartphones, metros, malls, overpasses etc that we don't realise that this country is mockingly seen as a third world nation. We take pride in every small achievement of our country, but we never hang our head in shame when the nation loses every time — when a child begs out on the streets.

The Curious Case of Mental Health in India

Mental health care is always a topic that is not yet fully has become a topic casual conversation in the world – in India it is far from becoming a discussion topic in our homes. Maybe it is the sheer ignorance or just the lacking the capacity recognise someone's problems – mental health in India is synonymous with *pagal khana* (mental asylum).

According to the older generation of parents – depression is just a made up thing – if you are depressed – they give you the most unique and the most absurd solution for it – just don't overthink and start being happy. If you are further persistent that you are depressed or having suicidal thoughts, they will start drawing comparison that how your life is so better than most of the people living in India. It all comes down to this sheer fact in India that if you have a roof over your head, clothes on your body and a belly filled with hot meals three times a day, then you shouldn't have the audacity to voice any type of concerns. In India it has always been about survival – getting yourself a source of income, then a house and then a family – no time for individual aspirations, just the satisfaction, you are not on the road like the millions begging for the basic necessities. Here to open a discussion about being unhappy and being depressed gets shunned by the society's skewed viewpoint – it is a problem for the poor who fights for the bread and the rich who have all the money to spend on an expensive psychiatrist; what about the middle class? They can't be depressed – because they are rich enough to not being homeless and poor enough to afford quality mental health care.

Mental health has always been the point of ridicule in India – a country where misogyny is as casual as it gets – being a man and being depressed is the worst thing you can do for yourself – either you'll be classified as mad (in a very harsh terminology) or being taunted for stop being a little girl. Mental health care is as far being recognised as a problem to address here in India. The country is plagued with menacing poverty, political corruption and struggling to address individual liberties that mental health care takes a backseat. India is currently, one of the most depressed countries in the world, ranking fifth and following this suit, it is one of the largest contributors to suicide deaths.

In a nutshell, depression isn't just made up or is a straight up problem where you need to send someone to a mental hospital but something you need to address and then take care of it. It can't be helped, if you undermine by saying that it is just the problems of the poor and the rich.

Now, let's push the debate a little further and talk about another such topic that on the contrary gets the attention but in a very negative way – homosexuality.

LGBT and India

When the Britishers ruled us, they introduced their form law to us. They laid the foundation for almost all Indian laws. In the modern era, we somehow find ourselves following the antiquated colonial laws of the British. A shining example of such is the infamous section 377 of the IPC which in a way criminalised homosexuality by curbing sexual nature of the relationship. Homosexuality was decriminalised in a Delhi High court verdict which in 2013 was reversed by the Supreme Court. The support of section 377 which indirectly criminalised homosexuality opened up a debate in the country. The liberal faction of the country spoke in favour of the right to one's sexual preference and the other more conservative faction supported such a verdict. The country that is deeply religious has always seen homosexuality as a disease but not a fundamental sexual preference. Maybe the homophobia is due to unawareness, ignorance and blindly following religion. Politicians and influential babas claim that its a mental disease and should be cured of; one very famous baba even made a claim that he can cure homosexuality.

The country remains in ignorance and while the major democracies have accepted homosexuality and LGBT rights as fundamental and rudimentary. Population in the urban spheres have somehow learned the reality of homosexuality but the overwhelming majority of the country is in deep homophobia. In India, homosexuality is regarded as something vile, disgusting and unnatural. Why is it so? The deep-rooted fear and homophobia that makes people believe that anyone who is gay is a sexual predator on the loose; a gay man can sexually assault anyone and can turn them like him. To counter such wonderful argument, I would ask you to consider this — if a man is straight and is only sexually attracted to women, then does it mean that he would go on sexually assaulting any woman that he encounters; and if someone does sexually assault anyone, then it's a crime and is not an appropriate behaviour. Similarly, any gay man who exhibits inappropriate sexual misconduct is a criminal and will be prosecuted in a similar fashion as a straight man with any form of sexual misdemeanours.

The idea of your child being gay is unfathomable to parents. They believe its a phase and in India, we have seen many cases where gay men and women are married off in a pretence that they are straight. These marriages suffer and there is little or no sexual relationship amongst the couples. The fear of societal backlash and feeling that being gay is a sin can even make gay men and women suicidal. Parents and the general public wonders why a gay man can't have sexual interest in a woman and similar for a lesbian. Now, if you are a straight man, if I force you to develop a sexual attraction towards a man rather than a woman, how would you react? You would obviously feel disgusted and would feel violated; similarly, a gay man would feel similarly for a proposed sexual relationship with a woman as unnatural and gross. Homosexuality is not a choice like selecting one's wardrobe but a way you are born as; your sexual preference stems from your biological built rather than you choosing homosexuality as a lifestyle. Sexual needs come under the basic necessities like food and water according to American psychologist Maslow; and to deny the sexual preference of a human being is a violation of basic human rights.

People belonging to the LGBT community often find themselves as objects of ridicule in society and are ostracised from the mainstream society. The segregated communities in India are known as hijras; these transgender population lives in separate communities and are more or less engaged in a profession given to them by the society. A gay man or a woman can hide his or her sexual preference and can lead a normal life by pretending to be straight. They can live amongst the inner circle of the society and can hold normal day jobs but hijras don't find themselves in such a luxury. Their visible difference in appearance are red flags for people to treat them normally, and that's why they live in separate niche communities and are occupied in certain niche occupations. Almost no one would give a normal day job to a transgender or be comfortable around them. They incite fear and makes them a peculiar part of the normal society of two genders. The discrimination that they face is evident in their treatment by police and the common folks. They are often denied medical services — doctors refusing to see them. Their community either have to engage in prostitution or rely on begging. Because of this HIV numbers are high in such communities.

Indian Film Industry

One of the mainstream sub-genre of comedy in India for years had been cross-dressing — particularly done by males. Every big actor has done it to get easy laughs from the audiences. Television shows have exploited male cross-dressing comedy sub-genre to such an extent that some male actors are more easily recognised in their cross-dressing avatar rather than their real masculine ones. Now a gay man would be stereotyped heavily, and it is very common in films and television to portray gay characters as potentially perverted and comical. From big-name celebrities to comics on television everyone has played a stereotyped gay character to get laughs. Gay characters are portrayed as overly feminine men who get aroused easily when they lay an eye another man; these gay men would try to woo other men. A gay character in Indian movies and television is always showcased as a sexually motivated feminine man.

Movies and television are such powerful mediums that they can teach people about events, places and other people through their real or stereotyped portrayal. If a gay man is portrayed as a normal man with real-life problems and anecdotes, then Indian people would have a different outlook on homosexuality. Yes, a gay man can have feminine characteristics, but it doesn't make them sexual predators out on the loose. Television and film industries in India needs to grow up start portraying gay men and women in more realistic terms and they can take a cue from Hollywood who knows how to handle LGBT portrayal on screen.

Film industry of our country

Indians are an ardent lover of cinema; we are the largest producer of movies in the world; we are a nation that has numerous regional film and television industries catering to a variety of language speakers from North to South and East to West. India has a majority population speaking Hindi (mainly northern part of the country) and that is why Hindi Film Industry such as Bollywood is considered the focal point of Indian cinema. It is mainstream and it is what ignorant people consider to be Indian cinema in its purity. The cinematic content of quality does get produced in our country but still we find ourselves in a struggling quest for quality cinematic standing in the world. No one at the world stage, takes our cinema seriously, which is evident from the fact that we win almost as little glory as small nations with no cinematic roots. Our people have this insane love for films, which can be assessed from the hero worshipping of actors and actresses; people down south take this hero worshipping to another level by comparing their beloved actors to gods and goddesses. In India, either you live to see yourself become a hero who is worshipped by all despite visible vices or a nobody who is ignored despite all the virtues.

Our film industry relies on a weird formula of escapism and larger than life elements. It portrays a hunky masculine male actor as the epitome of all that is good. He can fight off almost all the villain that you can put in front of him; he is motivated to all this because of his love interest: the female actor who is put out in the display for either lust or traditional love. She is a side piece with no character development, individuality and aspirations. She is there to look good, appeal to our hero and dance precisely to the tunes of numerous songs that are inserted at the expense of disrupting the flow of the movie. It is quite

49

ignorant to say that all movies run on such a formula but it will be highly ignorant to say that majority doesn't, because they do. Popular actor tends to be the ones who are well over the fifties and romances actresses half their age onscreen; sexism comes into play here. Actresses over forty often find themselves unemployed and actors over fifties find them playing teenage heartthrobs. To say that our film industry is a business which rakes in profit despite its bad quality products is kind of a brief summary. When you look at Hollywood, European cinematic endeavours and even our Asiatic counterparts, we see film industries constantly looking to push the envelope. Yes, they have their fair share of bad cinema but the majority is overwhelmingly creative, engaging and maturely handled that alludes Indian cinematic principles. We are a badly run cinematic country with flimsy morals and eye for gold. We are a country that makes sexism casual through cinema; our movies show our hypocrisy: sex is a taboo topic of discussion in our daily lives but in a contradictory fashion, we dance to the popular tunes of softcore pornographic-esque item songs.

The film industry finds itself creating one movie after another that is laced with unneeded songs and bad storylines. Does the country of almost one and a half billion souls only know about romance and singing and dancing around a tree? There are filmmakers who are telling stories that are true to their core and tells the story of our country, but they often find themselves out of the mainstream. Stories of boy meets girls, fights off goons and all goes well is escapism and not what the growing section of the educated young population wants. There is often a weird feeling that people just go to watch movies in a bid to escape from the realities of life. Movies are for entertainment but they necessarily don't have to be parallel to the ground reality. People want movies that are creative, well-acted and relatable. To please the lowest common denominator, film industry is pushing the educated young population to find solace in foreign films. I feel ashamed when I see foreigners making movies on our Indian icons like Gandhi, Ramanujan and many others, while we sit on our mediocrity and deciding which superstar movie we'll watch during the festive season. Again, the idea of Indian lives, sensibilities and relatability is alluded from mainstream Hindi cinema. There are many regional industries who are vying for attention and making content that is representative of India but is more or less side lined to the commercial glory and masala blockbuster formula. The South Indian film industry which comprises of Tamil, Telugu, Kannada and Malayalam language cinema is also a flourishing one and often gets the attention of the North as well. But sadly, like the Hindi counterpart, they too are trapped in a vicious circle mainstream appeasement and masala capers; again there are filmmakers catering to an educated urban youth or even highlighting the real issues of India, but they are exceptional cases and rarely find success.

Cinema is an artform that is representative of our culture and one medium that can have a direct impact on policymakers, social education and can highlight a crucial issue; to our disappointment, we are getting an endless brain-dulling factory produced films that are of no real substance and value. While other Asian countries are earning global recognition and are able to make the global audience connect with their culture, we are sitting in our own false sense of cinematic superiority and churning out movies that are laughable, embarrassing and aren't prominent enough to win an international stage laurel.

Indian Television Industry

One platform where you can see art die and mediocrity celebrated is Indian television. Everyone in our country knows how bad our television is; the television industry is a synonym to bad acting, storyline, visual effects and plot twists. Indian television industry is tenfold worse than our film industry; you can imagine the level of quality our Indian television produces.

First let's talk about the initial days of the television: the days of good old Doordarshan, that in its olden days churned good quality shows with a moral compass and an entertainment quotient. As globalisation seeped in, we saw television becoming a household affair in the late 90s and thus began the rise of private entertainment channels. At first the family saga revolving around kitchen wars in a gigantic (preferably Gujarati household) took centre stage. One of the most popular shows in Indian television history was *Kyunki Saas Bhi Kabhi Bahu Thi* which roughly translates to *Because Mother in Law was also Once a New Bride.* The show was a revelation at that time and paved the way for years of bad television content. Similarly, these soap operas revolving around females in the house were all the rage; they ran five days a week with a runtime of almost half an hour. They all have similarities: heavy sexism made casual, a patriarchal structure where women were restricted to kitchens and men worked outside and melodrama of incomprehensible proportion. These shows never had seasons and exhausted its users with all its character changes and inexplicable death and rebirth of its characters. Mihir Virani became a household name synonym to plastic surgery; so, if the main actor got in a tiff with the show's makers, then they would kill him/her off and brought the character back from dead with a new face, thanks to amazing plastic surgery. The point of these shows were opposite of cinematic art but rather poorly produced mass consumption commodities. These shows back then and even in the modern day and age don't have a soul, relatability quotient and developed a severe aversion to logic.

If we move on from the badly produced soap operas, then we enter the realm of the cringe-worthy world of reality television shows. Reality shows are cringe-worthy all over the world, with few exceptions. They rely on emotional exaggeration and manipulation to get heavy viewership and fan base. In India, the emotional quotient is dialled up to a notch of exaggerated proportion. There are reality shows about singing, dancing, acting, talent and comedy; these shows follow the same procedure: washed up celebrities as their judges; peppy television anchors who are always smiling; auditions taking place all over the country prompting starry-eyed simpleton standing in queues of hours. These auditions are televised selling the hopes of being India's next superstar; they show certain clips of either handful of talented men and women and some with a bad audition that judges laugh at and in turn we laugh at. Then we come at the main stage, where it's all about poverty porn these days. There are montages about every contestant — how they are from a poor family and overcame tough situations. After every performance, either it's a judge crying or the contestant crying or the parent crying, and this cues for a very cringe-inducing editing: sad music in the background and slow motion of the crying person. The emotional element is squeezed dry until the audience feels enchanted by it. This is classic manipulation of audiences making them feel that there is a reality in these reality shows. To be honest reality shows are scripted and mass-produced commodities, with the sole intent of garnering viewership through emotional manipulation. The worst part is that these days reality shows are centred around kids these days. There are kids who can sing, dance and act; they become the golden eggs for their parents to cash in on. These shows have a gruelling schedule that make a kid's life miserable. Little kids don't really have a clue what's happening and are happy with the audience's applause. They don't have an iota of a clue that their parents and channels producers are earning money out of their talent and visible innocence that captivates audiences. Psychologically, these kids feel no need of formal education and often finds themselves robbed of a normal childhood. This can have a severe impact on their future, as at such a little age, they taste success and fame. Some parents are such monsters that they grind their children to train mercilessly; again, tried and tested notions of parents' emotions towards their children and vice versa to rake in more views. These shows don't really find a need to end the show quickly, but stretch them to an endless proportion. The aim of the show is never finding the real talent but just making a show that gains a good viewership and rakes in big moolah.

When we are exploiting little kids for entertainment and money, then there is something fundamentally wrong in the society. Indian television has an ugly side, that everyone ignores, no one is willing to support good content, all of them are suppressed by censor that makes sex, religion and frankly any real issue as taboo. The masses believe that this is the highest a content can get and gullible minds take in what this idiot box shows them. Television is one influential medium and sadly it has become rotten and Indian television shines in this rotten state of affairs.

Offence R Us

Ours is a country of people with different sensibilities and social understanding but yes there is a but – that offence has lost its meaning. Let me explain. There is a line between what is appropriate and what is not. For some a banana can be seen as a non-offensive fruit and to some it can appear to resemble as a phallic shaped object that resembles male genitalia and that's how perception works. Different people see things differently. Now similar to the lines of perception in context and this is the most important of all. If someone made a joke on let's say a popular politician with a context that obviously meant to elicit laughs and not insults, then should we take offence to it? Let's say I make fun of my mother, does it give any other person in the world a right to take offence that it might have had hurt my mother's sentiments? Now let's take it to a deeper level, if someone jokes on race, colour and nationality, is it offensive? The answer is a resounding 'No'. But you ask why isn't it offensive? Because CONTEXT matters. When you are poking fun with a clear context of just eliciting laughter, then it means you are not seriously insulting someone. The problem with us is that we take offence on things that are not offensive and are ambivalent about those things that are offensive.

Let me ask you this, why don't we take offence when someone urinates in public? Why don't we take offence by the fact that our roads and streets are filthy? Why don't we take offence when every other day we hear news of sexual abuse towards women in our country? Why don't we take offence on various sexist, racist and filthy statements made by our politicians every day?

Our offence is just reserved for very niche subjects and is wasted on things that aren't harmful and necessarily offensive.

How can a comedian threaten the moral fibre of our country? How can a little abusive language weaken our core values in our country in a movie?

Do you see a pattern here – just to justify this notion that we need to protect our country – we are curbing a basic right to freedom and healthy dissent but forgetting what the setbacks that are stopping our country really are. No healthy discussion about sexual well-being or a satirical urban act can push this country of strong identity but weaken it is these ignorant and gullible violent pricks who have conveniently place themselves as the moral police and authority of what is offensive and what is not. Now let's talk about taking offence online – which has gotten way uglier these days. The most astonishing thing is the things people take offence to and sometimes it feels they take offence on someone else's behalf. One of the most infamous cases where a popular comedian recorded a silly conversation by using one of the many snapchat filters between two of India's most well known public figures. Now here what happened was people on behalf of these two well-known public figure came forward and took offence on their behalf. At first, I thought this snapchat video must have had something very insulting or something outright threatening to somebody's life or else people are not that stupid to file FIR but sadly I was mistaken. The video had this comedian just poke fun at these public figures and impersonate them. Now what the debate should have had been that if the people found it funny or not? Yes, you have freedom of expression to call out that it wasn't funny or in good humour but in no way it should be seen as a criminal offence. In our country women are often casually threatened with rape and other physical abuses and no one takes offence. This is where you see an intent of criminal activity, yet no one bats an eye here. Basically, the ones taking offences in the name of the country or their politician or well-known public figures either don't get the context or just find it an easier path for instant recognition.

The irony is that the comedians who are in fact are someone not to be taken seriously at first place are taken seriously and the politician who are to be taken seriously on their words can utter the most offensive or insensitive remarks, yet no one seems to get offended there. There is no hurt sentiment, or it is against Indian culture but rather just the doings of people with far less common sense to comprehend the satire and the context behind things. These online haters or commonly known as trolls are either blind followers of some form of ideology and have political biases and would look at every nook and corner of the Internet to bully a citizen with his/her right to show his/her displeasure with any political entity.

It is a sad state of affair that jokes done purely out of entertainment value are getting all the wrong attention compared to daily threats of death and sexual abuse to people of opinions. Offence should be taken but not in a way that jeopardises democracy and is biased for a particular political agenda that thrives on preserving a definition of Indian culture that has become archaic a long while ago.

Religious sentiments are never about actual hurt but are just a way of reminding the power control of religious institutions or a visible vote bank or a clear group of radicals to side with. In comparison to all of this, why don't we see the learned scholars versed in religious to react vehemently? If there is a genuine ground for hurting one's religious sentiments, then a civil discourse of Judiciary or even voicing one's opinions through social media or other forms can be considered. The vigilante type of mob justice is never out of deep introspection or genuine hurt. No one really cares and knows the reason for one's offence. Someone said that something is bad, the passive religious militias get triggered and come alive in action. Such radical religious and cultural organisations are filled with unemployed and propaganda induced youth that are ready to get triggered anywhere and with anything. It's basically

57

internet tolls coming to life; they would protest against any movie, song, play, art and show that comes under their scanner, when convenient to the one pulling the strings. Many movies with controversial materials fly off the radar, while due to unfortunate timings (mostly during an election or something) some movies with no real controversial punch suffers pangs of the religious uprising.

Genuine and peaceful religious debates are rare these days. India is modelled over peaceful coexistence not petty polarisation of its people of different faiths. The intelligent and the employed population doesn't really care about unnecessary protests over a harmless movie or any art form expressing its creator's opinions. The ground reality is that things should really offend people in India never really gets protested or talked about religious groups or political factions. They don't really care about the problems plaguing Indian masses; there is no protest anytime soon over rising air pollution in various Indian cities; there is no offence taken to the rise in the number of sex crimes in the country; in general, offence in India is reserved for petty and useless things. You can also see the stark difference between protests done by intelligent, educated and well-meaning citizens of India compared to the damage done to public properties, handing out death threats and vile behaviour displayed by political and religious fanatics. India's problem is the growing population of unemployed youth who gets swayed easily by hate propaganda; with a blindfold over their eyes, they believe in every lie that's been told to them. India seems to take offence at everything out there and it's hurting the country deeply and shedding its democracy slowly.

Religion > Logic

In a country where we have people of different faiths, institutions and beliefs, we have one thing in common—a heightened sense of religious insecurities. The belief that my religion is more morally upright than yours and anything said against our religion is blasphemy of the highest kind, can be seen and felt in India; when I am talking about religion, I am not speaking particularly about Hindus or Muslim, but about every religion that has followers with less logic in their arguments and more hatred in their speeches. Religion in India has now become an effective tool for politicians to polarise populations and create vote banks; they are also very convenient way for pseudo spiritual gurus who preach their followers and very smartly pitches it in a spectacular business model— the various ashrams and temples (state of the art) and the spectacular amount of money that needs to be spent on various religious artefacts is something similar to a great businessman. Religion, as I believe was invented to bring together a community of people who can work together and can have spiritual understandings of life as we know it, but when exploited by sly men, it became a tool to rule people through fear and fake information.

In our country, if someone creates a hoax, it spreads like wildfire. The hoax can be in the form of certain idol of a god is either drinking something or something miraculous happened. The blind followers get sold on it; just see the amount of money collection, these big temples sweep in—now if it isn't a business model, then what is it? I have no problem with whatever belief system someone carries but when someone goes to a religious institute and spends lavishly in the form of offerings, priest's tips and other mumbo jumbo, then the logic is defied. I have seen people who are highly educated and logical bows down to religion, no one questions the motives of the self-proclaimed godmen because of this insane fear that has been instilled in every one of us, that if we speak anything bad against our gods, something bad or ominous will happen to us. So, in a way we believe that God is so petty that he/she/they will take revenge on us, if we question anything?

The online atmosphere of hate

To be apolitical or even a less opinionated being is more of a safe bet in this world; similarly, Indian have been bitten by the bug of turning any form of socially relevant discussion into an ugly and vile argument in online social media platforms. First of all, this mostly American way of dividing the voting population into liberals and conservatives have seeped into Indian conscience (thanks to the media). Like in the USA, where liberal and conservative media, supporters and ideas are at loggerheads with each other — similarly India is being cleaved into what is liberals and conservatives. Traditionally there is right and left in politics — each calling each other names — extreme of both are either communist or fascist. The right calls the left as libtards, Congressi and communist; the left chides the right by calling them bhakts, sanghis and fascists. When you start seeing the voting population with different ideas as part of different camps — you effectively see a deep divide — this is glorified by the media on each spectrum. What happens here is that media supporting the left or the right ideology and starts classifying citizens in these two political directions — which helps politician lure people to vote for them by classifying themselves as the saviour of the right or left ideology. Media — the exaggeration machine of this new age starts fanning the mild fire — instigating people on both spectrums.

Enters the cyberspace — online social media platforms like Twitter, Facebook etc making a very basic political idea volatile enough to start a war of words. Internet trolls waiting in a corner with already typed abuses and cuss words thrives on toxic social media debates. Any issue that is political in nature soon converts into a war amongst people who support different political ideologies. No one is interested in understanding that we live in a diverse country and every citizen wants a good life for themselves; everyone's definition of a good life is different and the country must accommodate these ideas but we have been divided so decisively by politicians, media and various spokesperson who offers think pieces that we find hating each other much easier than working with each other.

There are hateful jingoistic pages — where Hindus discuss how to eliminate all the Muslims and the Muslims discuss the vice-versa; these type of pages and communities on social media which polarises a country that has been living with open hearts and a community where temple and mosques are standing at an arm's length is very shameful. The notion that it is easy to hate each other is a cause for more conflict and undermining the ideas of love and living in harmony; you might wonder that such idealistic lip service is for the talks, but it is a reality that has been lived in a country that had always been proud in showcasing its cultural and religious diversity. Casting secularism in a bad light in online platforms by thrusting and sharing false and fake news to instigate hate is new age terrorism; for me terrorism isn't just the physical act of hate but also the instigation of communities against others.

I like to believe people still prefer love over hatred; the online atmosphere is not conducive for rational discussions but only fanning the fire of hatred; trolling and fighting with each other has become so easy online due to anonymity. What I am trying to say is — stop calling yourself the left or the right — but rather respect the democracy that our country is. If someone is religious and patriotic — it doesn't mean it's fascism; similarly if someone is an atheist or secular or not boasting patriotism — it doesn't mean it's communism. Respect each other's views and let's start working together to decide a course of action that can run through deliberate and civil discussions rather than the vile hurling abuses that is common to both online cyberspace and within our Parliaments.

The problem here is that we all want to address a problem in a way that it pleases our intellectual ability — now let's talk about a self-professed college educated liberal and a small businessman who is a religious conservative — both of them would differ from each other in every single standpoint — but both would effectively ignore the core problems of this country. These both politically apart gentlemen would ignore the uncountable men, women and children on the streets begging — who are hungry, malnourished and suffering — these gentlemen would only argue with each other and not being interested in basic problems that are haunting our country. Poverty doesn't require a left or a right approach, it needs proactive stance which is hidden cleverly by pitting one side with each other; thanks to social media, the people who are doing work to address the problems are overshadowed by the abuses of libtards, bhakts and anti-nationals.

This country doesn't need left or right ideology; this country needs to address basic problems such as poverty, overpopulation, unemployment, education, healthcare, women's safety etc. rather than discussing whether you are a BJP or Congress or Banana or Apple party supporter. Let's make online social debates to come in full circle discussing ways to eradicate these problems rather than making it a breeding ground for hatred and division.

We wait until the problem gets even bigger

From the example of air pollution in Delhi to every mosquito related outbreak, we can sense one clear pattern, that the actions in this country are only taken when shit hits the fan. The air became bad and no one batted an eye; the air grew a little worse, still we slept like babies; the air grew so worse that the whole world took notice, and this gave us a wakeup call to address this problem. The Delhi air pollution menace is one of the shining gems of the many public related health risks that could have been avoided easily but inept governance and an ignorant civic attitude pushed a minor threat to become a major one.

Mosquito-related diseases which are just synonym to third world countries are being eradicated from almost every other nation who gives a damn about their citizens. Our neighbouring countries has mosquito-related diseases at bay, yet we all struggle in India. Japanese elephantiasis, dengue, chikungunya and many other potentially deadly diseases are spread by mosquitoes. In India, come winter and we welcome mosquitos wholeheartedly. Centre lays out plans, there are advertisements and camps from state government all for PR sake. The problem in India lies that we actually don't give a flying damn about our citizens. The citizens have been accustomed to believing that in a country of men and women to a jaw-dropping excess, the life of one isn't of much worth.

The middle class at least has the awareness, and the necessary attention to such problems, so that they can avoid such health hazards. That leaves to the poor denizens, that are the majority of this country. They are just seen as: vote banks according to the politicians; labourers and domestic servants for the middle class and criminals for the justice system. Any health-related epidemic finds its ground zero in these men and women who live in surroundings that invite diseases of all kinds. The problem here is that until and unless the middle class or the upper middle class suffers, no one cares and declares a public health crisis. The Delhi air pollution reached a severe level that can be compared to the consumption of at least 50 cigarettes a day. Now, this affected all strata of the population, that's why it garnered media attention and hence the politicians came under fire.

In India, people living in slums and dirty surroundings die, suffer and invite forms of diseases and illness that would make a sophisticated nation ashamed of itself. People suffer every day, wait in lines in the corrupt, inefficient and dilapidated government hospitals; no one cares just yet. Unless it's a public health crisis that affects the affluent, we as a country close our eyes and forget about most of our population that is suffering and have accepted the fact that their worth as a human in a country like ours is lower than the holy cow (which is worshipped, taken care of and respected).

Cringeworthy News Channels

Like our film and television industry, news channels also have a serious aversion to professionalism and quality content. The news channels in India are one of the most cringe-worthy things you can encounter in your life. Bad visuals, horrific video editing and repeating a news over 1000 of times. I know that news channels all over the world don't really have a stellar reputation but Indian news channel are on whole other level. Indian news channel feels like a documentary style soap opera that Indian entertainment channels seem to churn quite magnificently.

From covering serious news to covering something that shouldn't count as news, we can simply see the master unprofessionalism in the news anchors conduct (there are a few exceptions), the choices of clickbait headlines and the ironically comedic voice-over that seems to worsen the already inserted bad video effects. That's why people in India are losing faith in the authenticity of Indian news channels. News channels in India have notorious reputation; there is obvious political bias, over sensationalising a simple topic and aversion from fact-checking. All this makes news watching experience a drab and frankly it's making people less informed and dumber. There are again a few exceptions out there and there are some channels that are investing in good journalism, fact checking and neutral news coverage.

When the news channels of such national coverage have corny graphics, pathetic journalism and cutthroat competitiveness just to present a news first, then we have got a problem at hand. The media has the power to question political overlords, initiate social change and bring out stories that people are quite ignorant about; Indian media does the opposite: they pander to political overlords, initiate select social changes and bring out only mainstream stories. The news channel oozes of stupidity, ignorance and frankly appears to be drunk in its own power of broadcasting. If only news channel behaved seriously and not become the second choice of soap opera fans, then we might have a chance in educating the masses on important issues of our country.

I feel newspapers in our country still have some integrity intact, and news channels frankly can learn something from it. News channels are busy churning out saucy ghost stories to be telecast at night slots; they are busy creating a political drama amongst affluent politicians; they are more interested in celebrities' lives; they are more interested in TRPs; they aren't interested in serious news coverage.

Why do the news channels consider the audiences moron? Why do these news channels only worry about the sensationalisation and entertainment value in a news story? Such questions are asked every day yet they fall on deaf ears. These news channels are propagating ill-researched stories, misconstruing statements and shifting their political allegiances every day.

Like the American version of Fox news, which is right leaning news agency, we have many such news channels fashioned upon that model. There are also left-leaning news channels in India to counter a heavily biased right centric media of our country. The point here is: why news channels feel the need to align themselves with any political spectrum? They are at the centre or they are a neutral spectator of the society. Why do we have discussions, when one news channel praise BJP, then its right-wing news channel and when one praise congress or any left party, then its left-leaning news channel. Why can't news channels operate at the centre of things? Let them praise and criticise on their accord without giving them a tag. Modern day example is the good old Doordarshan News channel, but sadly it has viewer base that isn't a faction to these catchy and soap opera-esque mainstream news channels. It's always been known that media is biased; there are some free speech advocates and hard-hitting journalism that shines, but in an overall picture, it's the vile, obnoxious, intelligence hampering and mass catering news circulation that is popular at this moment.

It was Arnab Goswami, who brought the entertainment quotient in the houses of ordinary people who flipped through a plethora of entertainment as well as news channels. Entertainment channels are mostly fiction and less relatable, but what news channels are offering is real men and women venting out hatred and frustration in a live telecast circus-like debate with an opinionated ringmaster at the top. I am not gonna give him the credit of being a journalist; he is at best a showman and master orator who runs a reality television show on his supposed news channels. When you break down any mainstream Indian news channel, you can clearly see a pattern. There is same news that is being repeated throughout the day; the same news that was broadcasted in the afternoon, repeats with a more captivating headline (BREAKING NEWS— the most casually used term in the news world). The prime time that is 9 p.m. at night is the main stage for the star orators to come out and play. Throughout this prime news, we see accusations being made, biased opinions foretold, facts largely ignored and entertainment for the audiences who had just came home from work. There are guests of all kinds invited to such news cum entertainment shows: religious fanatics, political parties' spokesperson, opinionated celebrities and worn out political pundits. Either they are pitted against each other in a debate that doesn't make sense or just straight out noise fest or they are pushed by the news anchors to get something controversial out of their mouths. A simple topic at hand gets so badly treated that it loses its worth; the viewers at home stop caring about it because all the entertainment has been juiced out to a maximum by the news channels.

News channels have biases and are mainly ignorant of their conduct. We had Uttar Pradesh elections and from morning to the end of the night — we had the same cycle of Uttar Pradesh election drama. These continued for months ignoring other parts of the country; ignoring the plight of various people across the land and moreover ignoring the responsibility of being a fair and righteous presenter of the news that matters.

Let's talk about the cringe-worthy part of the news channels; we had horrible graphics, vile anchors instigating mass hysteria and sensationalising simplest of matters. The afternoon and the late-night slots of the news channels are the most cringiest content you can come across (and I am saying this even though the majority of Indian television content is cringefest). Afternoon slots are dedicated to celebrities or to be more fair hero worshipping. With a token female anchor with excited demeanour and fake accent — whose job is to tell what the celebrities eat; how they party; whom do they date; where are they holidaying and what kind of pranks do they pull on each other. Well, that's pure news for you all. To dive straight into cringe festivities, we look at the 11 p.m. fest, which I like to call as crime porn. Every news channel has a shady character with menacing looks and baritone-esque voice to act as bogeyman with a teleprompter. They pick crime news from a buffet of murder, rape, robbery etc and narrate this story creating it as dramatic as possible.

News channels have the habit of making celebrities out of morally skewed people and denouncing righteous people and making them public enemies. News channels only want to bask in the glory of sporting achievements with continuous circle jerking of mainly cricketers but when they underperform, news channels are the first one to throw them under the buses. News channels bring out the opinions of deranged individuals and airing them for impressionable audiences. News channels influence everyone; they confirm false fears; they help create botched up political opinions of young people. News channels have a heavy responsibility towards the society, but they behave and operate in a purely biased way and project themselves as a centre for reality entertainment.

Though we are seeing a change — thanks to the easy access of the Internet, where the not so gullible people rather subscribe to intelligent online creators who present the news as it is. But the reach of national television is far greater and have a huge impact on opinion formulations; online creators are doing what they can but to counter them, armies of political trolls and certain political party affiliates are constantly harassing and bullying them. When you become honest, it doesn't play down well because we are conditioned to see and hear the biased rendering of facts and opinions in this country.

The Peculiar Indian Society

The '*Chalta hai*' attitude of the Indian society

There is an attitude that is prevalent across this country and that is '*chalta hai*' attitude which roughly translates to 'yeah fine' and this attitude is alright and quite needed in some aspects of life but if this attitude becomes a common part of life, then it's just masquerading laziness. In India, if something is broken, fixing it or investing in maintenance is never an option but let's just ignore the broken roads and infrastructure and move on around it; now this lax attitude of ignoring a problem has paved the way for another Indian system of jugaad which similar to chalta hai is very handy in certain situations but if inculcated as part of one's habit, then quite harmful. Jugaad is basically finding temporary solutions to a problem; jugaad is basically how to fix a broken thing for a certain amount of time to delay any investment into buying its replacement or such. To see beautiful shining examples of Indian jugaads, just take a stroll down the Indian roads and you will find people with brilliant innovations— from motorised hand puller to wooden planks laid down to cover the gaps between roads. To be fair, our chalta hai attitude is a direct result of corruption. If our roads get broken, then it would take government officials considerable amount of time to fix it, in that period of time, so many grave accidents could have or might have had happened. People of this country are experiencing government failures for so many years, that in an instinct of survival we have to be more chalta hai and jugaad enforcers. In a country, where basic public facilities are rare such as dustbins, functioning red lights and proper footpaths for pedestrians, then the citizens wouldn't know what are the rules of basic decorum. So, if you throw garbage on the road, then it's chalta hai; if you are riding a bike without a helmet, then chalta hai; if you break a red light, then it's chalta hai. This collective attitude of adjusting and chalta hai is not something a citizen of a developed country would even appreciate. This attitude of ours where we don't give a damn about anyone else's concerns than just ours have made a society with a very low level of civic sense. In India you could park in such a way that it occupies half of the road; In India you can make a U turn in a highway; In India you can throw any garbage anywhere; In India, you can urinate at any spot as per your heart's desire; In India, if you are a dairy farmer, you can leave your life stock at the middle of the road causing hours of traffic jam; In India you can open up your street side food or vegetable stalls, occupying half the roads; In India, you can pay bribe to any of the government or police officials to get your work done; In India you can play loud music on speakers in residential areas at late nights; In India you can go on and be inflict casual racism; In India, it is a common experience for women and girls to get stared at and grope at public spaces; In India it is quite common to see patriarchy at play where boys are almost always free to do whatever their heart desires and girls....well not so much; In India, you can have domestic help at rates cheaper than standard minimum wages that are established all around the globe; In India you can create public nuisance without the fear of any strict action; In India, it is common to see little children begging for money on the roads and it is a well-known fact that these children are being recruited by human traffickers forcing them to beg on the roads; In India, it is quite common to wake up in the morning to read in the papers that another minor got raped or sexually assaulted; In India it is quite common information that all are represented electives have past criminal records or case pending in the courts; In India, the courts are inefficient and have the largest number of pending cases in the world; In India, the civic sense of common public is so low, that if by a miracle government thinks of bringing out some new infrastructure, it gets badly annihilated by the common public.

In a nutshell, India has now comfortably adopted the chalta hai attitude because daily life of a citizen of India is so challenging that we have to bring out our survival instinct and just ignore the things that we see our wrong; the chalta hai attitude is seeped in so much, that kids in their houses don't expect that everything is to the standards of how western films show their normal middle classes live like; the chalta hai attitude is adopted by us and encouraged by our inept government of decades.

'*Log kya kahenge*' doesn't really make much sense

In India, if you hail from a middle-class family, then the first thing from the list of weird and illogical expectations or rather a straight up order from your parents would be to choose from two set of professions—being an engineer or a doctor; again, this is not the case for everyone, but yes overwhelming majority would definitely agree about this weird soft corner Indian parents have for engineering and medical professions. There is a very weird statement that most of the adults make when questioned by younger generation about choosing different forms of profession. Let's say, if you want to be a writer and you go on marching towards Indian parents to declare: I don't want to be an engineer! It is very likely that your parents would straight up say this set statement that I am sure any kid of my generation who bundled up enough courage to present a logical argument of why they don't want to be an engineer or a doctor has heard; the statement is, 'Log kya kahenge?' (What will people think?) Then this argument would be followed by you can be a writer/photographer/painter/filmmaker while being an engineer too and then they would go on giving some examples of so many famous writers, painters, filmmakers etc who were engineers and then became what they wanted to be. I don't understand why the hell do we have to put ourselves through an ordeal that we are not even remotely interested in? Why do parents want to waste their time, energy, resources and money on making us something that we clearly don't want to be? Why do parents think so low of creative career fields? Why do parents and the Indian society hellbent in brainwashing their children into believing that certain professions are superior to others?

76

I am baffled that Indian parents would gladly watch a new movie playing at the theatres but would hesitate when their children ask them if they could become a filmmaker or an actor; I am baffled that parents lovingly watch various sports and wouldn't encourage their children to pursue a career in sports; I am baffled that parents would appreciate music and dance forms but would hold their children's hand when they try to consider a full-fledged career in these fields. In our country, we don't lack talent and certainly have young gifted individuals but what we lack is the parenting backbone that is required by these fragile dreams of little children that breaks before even reaching its realisation. No offence meant to engineering as a profession, it is an essential part of society and a noble profession, but it has killed more dreams than it had helped realised. The country needs as many sportsperson, musicians, dancers, filmmakers and other artists as engineers, doctors and other traditional professions. This weird stigma attached that only children who are not intelligent go for arts and leaves science because they are afraid of working hard; so you meant to say that playing sports professionally doesn't require intelligence and hard work? Does playing a musical instrument in front of thousands with precision or singing impeccably at high decibels is as easy as it comes?

I can pose many such questions like these but still many would say that this is what corroding the youth of today; these liberal ideas and westernised norms are corrupting the minds of the young people of this country, who should be involved in a rat race of who scores more marks, who gets into IIT, who can work like a slave in a multinational company and who can make mummy and papa proud the most. So, if that's your vision of constructive and happy youth, then I want to be part of that corrupted youth that you hate and loathe so much, because that makes me happy and for me happiness trumps any form of hollow respect of relatives and neighbours around me.

You say it's my hobby, well I say it's my passion and no disrespect to the ones who are engineers or doctors, but if the argument is that life is much easier with a sturdy profession, then you are grossly wrong, people go through shit regardless of any profession they opt; that's life for you, it shits on you and rewards you when you work hard. So, teach your children to work hard and not be complacent but don't teach them engineering is the gateway ticket to happiness and prosperity, which it clearly isn't to be honest.

Coaching Classes and
Mass Production of Engineers

The most stressful time in a teenager's life is when he/she is forced to join a coaching class. These coaching classes are a multi-million dollar industries. In India, coaching classes for every sort of entrance test at graduation as well as postgraduate levels exist but the most notorious case is that of IIT-JEE coaching classes. A country of well over a billion souls with a sizeable young population either find themselves in poverty or if privileged enough to receive education, the end goal is to either be a doctor or an engineer. Coaching classes exploiting the hard-working parents that only believe engineering is their saviour; if they want to walk in the evening in their locality with their head held high — the only way is to make their child an engineer. In a society where subjects like Physics, Chemistry and Maths are considered far superior to subjects of arts and commerce, there is bound to be a doctrine where kids from an early age are spoon fed about this falsified dream of engineering being the only way to be successful and make their family proud. The moment, you step into high school, you find yourself in these coaching classes every day after school hours. Majority of these children are taught that only some years of hard work needs to be done and abandonment of their school life, teenage zest and any passion that they might have should be discarded in order to ace entrance exams and land a place at the coveted IIT. This is a pipe dream because the realistic chance of getting into an IIT is really slim. Let's do some simple mathematics, if 12 lakhs aspirants appear for the entrance exam and there are only about 10k seats and out of which only about 5k is reserved for general category, then what is the probability of getting into an IIT? It is as low as about 0.4 %. I know it's a tough competition but why are we enrolling those participants that clearly are not a fit for such a contest. Why are parents so hellbent in making their child an IITian? Why is engineering the only go to career option for the middle classes? Why coaching classes that are clearly business making entities thriving? Why there are so many engineering colleges springing up, operating like factories and churning out washed up engineers?

The situation never really gets addressed in this country. Why are we so hell-bent on producing engineers mercilessly? Everything boils down to one thing — respect in society. I don't really understand this Indian notion of respect and honour — if you are an IITian, you are almost considered as a royalty. Yes, you have a cracked a tough competition and have become an engineer with a stable job, but that doesn't make you an automatic candidate to earn my respect yet. All of the hard work you did was out of self-interest and that's fine. Your IIT degree doesn't make you a superior human being or will overshadow any of your bad traits. The point is that respect in society should be earned with the merits of social behaviour, etiquettes and doings, not on the basis of degrees. I will respect a person irrespective of his rocket science credential or liberal arts degree but on the basis of human quality. In India, education is limited to long hours of studying and clearing entrance exams; there is no stress on civic education or even stress on the importance of physical fitness, but only the enticing vision of medical and engineering colleges. Parents want to feel superior if their child is an engineer; so they can boast in front of their friends, colleagues and relatives who have their kids enrolled in supposed inferior by Indian standard — arts and commerce colleges. In India, getting in an IIT is not at all about learning engineering nuances and passion, but rather about socio-economic reasons. There will be a stable job and in the arrange marriage network— an IIT engineer, despite his flaws as a human being would be able to get the desired bride with a bag full of dowry goodies; sexism works in a mysterious way and in this IIT/engineering scenario — if a girl is a qualified engineer from IIT or any other prominent institute, then there would be less number of prospective groom available for her. This is because, she is now overqualified and boy's parents are intimidated by the fact that the girl is well educated and can earn as much or even more compared to their son.

Engineering is one profession that makes march ahead in the future; it's beautiful and extremely important for a progressive world but in India when you run colleges as factories that are producing a sea of engineers that are mediocre or have become engineers half-heartedly, then you are creating visibly frustrated, depressed and unemployed youth. In our country, jobs are plenty in the IT sector, and anyone who has for four years studied any other branch would eventually succumb and like a sheep in a herd join the mass recruitment of a multinational entity. People work better when they care about their work, by mass producing engineers in Indian society, we are hindering the efficiency of youth workforce. Let's make it a point where young child doesn't need to be forced into becoming an engineer or a doctor; these coaching classes and overzealous parents should talk about complexity of life and not brainwash children into thinking that engineering is their saviour and being an IITian is the ultimate goal towards happiness; because when these children would face the real-life situations, they would soon realise that engineering is not the only choice and way to happiness — they would loathe you and the whole system of Indian education. Coaching classes are clear cut money hungry corporations selling hollow dreams that engineering and medical profession are the only clear-cut ways for a happy life. Let your worldview grow and see that the modern world cares about talent not a brainwashed engineer; IITs are great but they are not the mecca for greatness; people rise up in their life because of their sheer talent, the conduct of themselves and the work they do. Let engineering be an option for a child who is genuinely interested, sees his/her future in it. Let children be talked with and guided about real life, rather than brainwashed by sinister coaching classes and frustrated parents who believe that engineering is the only noble profession out there. India is in a transition, there are lots of frustrated engineers who are beginning to realise the lies they were fed as a kid and how engineering has nothing to do with said success, respect and happiness. Thanks to social media and an exposure to a world of numerous career options, people are ditching the lies and opting for what they love. Even the coveted IItians are turning to the so-called inferior liberal arts and commerce. Let the lies die down and not besmirch this beautiful profession of engineering; let engineering be left with students who are passionate about it; let there be genuine colleges as opposed to horrendous money making colleges at every corner of the street; let coaching classes die down and pave the way for genuine teachers guiding passionate aspirants and let IIT be seen as an engineering college and not hailed as God's own creation because at the end of the day it's just a building.

The engineering colleges with the exception of some are mostly about mass producing students without stirring a sense of passion, love and career inkling towards their career pathways. Anyways the education system has always been like this where marks and class rank mattered but not the creative growth of a student. At colleges, it's all about scoring marks, pandering to professors and getting campus placements. Coaching classes prep a student for the entrance test without stirring any form of excitement regarding what being an engineer means. Now, when a student fresh out of a school — that taught him/her things that really isn't concrete enough to tackle real-life scenarios, faces a weird kind of a challenge. Parents, teachers and the society all shouted at the top of their voices that go out and become an engineer but failing to mention what an engineer does. Colleges just like the age-old Indian formula are interested in mugging from books and vomit it in the exam sheet. The real world is tough and engineering is not all the solution a kid needs. If you had foretold the real scenarios that passion should be left outside before entering an educational institution in India, then that would have been a help. Young men and women, enter college, hoping that being an engineer would be exciting and thrilling; little do they know that it's all about some mindless grind of endless examinations. The engineering colleges in India aren't interested in kindling the interest in engineering or as a matter of fact leap into big innovations. It's all about mass producing young men and women for multinational IT companies. We ask, why Indians aren't at the world stage in innovation and creative field? Well, at the world stage we prove to be hard workers; we excel at desk jobs and being model students. Throughout our schooling and college education, we only learn that creativity and passion are hobbies, while daily monotonous grind is a profession. The mass-produced engineers don't know shit about conjuring up innovations but are trained dogs to work at desk jobs. That's why in India, when someone goes through the soul-crushing experience of the engineering college, they latch on to their passions and changes their career directions. There are only a few souls, who love engineering enough to see it through the end and make something of themselves. The Indian mentality of education helps coaching classes extort large sums of money of preparing children to become future engineers who can work in IT companies for horrid pay and bitter life.

Student suicide: Two words that shouldn't be used in the same sentence

India ranks 24th in the global ranking in the highest number of suicides; for men the suicide rate is about 25.8 per 100,000 and 16.4 for women. Though, we may not be the country with the highest suicide rate but we are certainly becoming a country who is steadily climbing this ranking ladder. There are many reasons and population demographics that paints a very dark picture. Here, we will be mainly focusing on this weird increase in the number of student suicide. What makes a student go to such an extreme to end his or her life? There has to be something wrong with the education system, that students feel more comfortable in ending their lives rather than dealing with the problems they face at either at school or college.

In India, there is a very popular saying, which goes like this, '*Padhoge likhoge to banoge nawab, kheloge kudoge to hoge kharab*' *(If you study you will amount to something and if you play then you will amount to nothing.)* This is something every Indian kid have grown up listening either from their parents, grandparents or teachers. Education is a beautiful thing and is something that I highly endorse, but on the other hand thinking that education is only limited to books and exams is a gross misjudgement. Somehow, every teacher and parent in this country feels that education is all about scoring marks and cutthroat competition. Teachers are telling students to mug up whatever is written in their textbooks and parents doubling down on their children on studying day and night to score tremendous marks. Other forms of education that come from co-curricular activities and value system somehow takes a low priority stand to that of the traditional form of education that is trapped inside textbooks with a limited bound of knowledge.

The schooling system in India is all about how is better at remembering the same information from their textbooks and after that who can score better marks. Now, teachers act as a creator of fear, instilling this silly fear that if you don't score good marks then your 'future' will be finished; they also convince the overly protective parents about how their child is more interested in arts or other activities as opposed to scoring good marks. Now parents and teachers form a tag team, and like a rehearsed mantra, chants the word 'future' all the time. This makes a child wonder and even believe that scoring marks is the only way to be successful and make their parents as well as teachers happy. Some succeed in scoring good marks while the ones who just can't wrap their head around this concept or need of scoring marks to get educated, get booed collectively by society. The failures are made fun of by teachers, in ways of public shaming and when their parents get to know about their low marks, they also humiliate their own child in a way that is more personal and fearsome. Now, all this starts accumulating in a child— some just give up and start to succumb to this traditional system of education while others opt for a horrific method.

Students think that school is the only place that indoctrinates them; they look for college life, where they would be able to fulfill every desire that they always harboured; sadly, enters the reality of colleges. Most of the colleges in India, have their fair amount of teachers that shouldn't be allowed to exist in a 100 feet distance near a student, yet Indian colleges only hire on the basis of qualification not how they behave and handle students. A teacher is an integral part of a community, he or she is solely responsible for educating as well as imparting wisdom into young minds, yet the Indian education system hires people who just spew hatred and instill this horrible fear inside that of a student. This weird feeling that looms in the air where education has become a mixture of anxiety and fear. In India its all about forced education not about the correct education.

The purpose of an education is to make better citizens who are intelligent enough to choose their career and are capable enough in making important life decisions, yet education has just been reduced to scoring marks affair and blindly obeying what the educators have to say.

These frustrated individuals that are made school teachers and college professors who treat students in such a way that it shatters their confidence, self-esteem and a will to study. Suicide is something that is attempted when you feel that you are worthless and everything around you is negative and bad; student committing suicide is not normal; bad parenting and fearful education force the students to take their own life. It is always the fault of the environment, because no young student would end his or her life out of petty reasons; maybe for a teacher shaming a student is something that he/she does to get some kicks but you may never know how one small instigation can create a turmoil inside of someone. Our education system need teachers to be sensitive and soft-spoken rather than harsh, rude and treat students like dogs; parents should remember that to give birth to someone doesn't mean they owe you something that's why they have to study according to your own unrealistic expectations and be what you want them to be.

I cannot stress enough but to point out the haunting figures of young people killing themselves over stress that is loaned to them by their respective educational institutions. I agree that marks and academic pressure are something that does prepare a student about the life ahead but if this pressure reaches a point where it is not healthy and certainly not helpful — then it just creates havoc inside a student and makes him/her question his/her abilities. It is a scientific fact—when you exert pressure over carbon it becomes diamond but if you exceed beyond a point, you will only obtain dust. In India, bizarre way of lifestyle has been accepted, stringent of changing the trend, we embrace it as normal. For us, the things that are normal are quite bizarre for many people in other countries. If you are a student, then it is okay for you to be mentally harassed by your teachers and parents. Students in higher secondary school and more prominently in colleges go through the harshest form of mental harassment that it is dubbed as 'necessary evil' to teach them valuable lessons in life. An attitude, which the society has accepted is that whatever the teacher says is the truth and right while the student's voice is of less importance. In India, teachers can be insensitive, outright rude and hold personal vendettas against certain students; this not only makes student's life miserable but a feeling of helplessness looms. Every child in this country has been taught that it's okay to feel anxiety, stress and even depression, if it means getting your degree. You cannot correct an educator; you can't point out flaws in educator's conduct but can only sit there like an innocent lamb, accepting its fate. It's not normal for young students to feel the stress of highest orders; when fear encroaches your heart, it kills happiness, one's creative and analytical thinking and what seems of the world is a dark void of despair—hence the menacing suicide rates amongst our young crops. No one cares how creative you are; what bright future you hold but only the marks you score right now and whether you are able to bend backward to obey your educator's commands. The educators in our country, who are insensitive, corrupted and shouldn't be placed near ten feet to the kids are the ones in the majority and can be found in every schools and college of our country. So, it's not normal for a young student to feel anxiety, stress, depression and suicidal feelings owing to the untoward pressure by the educators and the society in general.

The Narrative of Elitism and '*Gawar*'

Britishers thrust their cultural superiority and made themselves feel superior to any native Indian. Britishers sold on this narrative that their way of life and especially their language is superior to Indian regional languages. The cunning strategy of making Indian feel inferior due to the colour of their skin, languages they spoke and the way of life they led. Indians were sold on this narrative and even today we believe in such skewed narration.

Elitist classes were created out of businessmen, politicians and intellectuals — that were subservient to the colonial masters and had resources to get acquainted with the British way of life and learn to converse in English fluently. The simpleton who was uneducated or even educated in the medium of their regional languages made the *gawars*. Gawar is an insult in Hindi for those who are either uneducated or bereted from urban customs or can't converse in English.

It has been 70 years since the colonial powers dissipated, but the elitist narration remained. Today, the one who can speak English is superior and the one who can't is inferior. It's not about the education qualification — you have garnered — but in which language you have garnered in. An English-speaking doctor is deemed more superior than a regional language speaking one; similarly in all walks and professions — the one speaking English is considered superior. In our schools and colleges — English teachers are more respected than the regional language teachers. The narration of English is superior has been troubling India for a while now. It's quite peculiar to see that India has more English speaker than the colonial power that sold this narrative.

I understand that English in a way is language franca of the world. It is one universal language that helps people from other countries communicate. But to see this language as superior to our Indian regional languages is absurd. I feel really weird when I see other countries feel proud of their own languages and learn English just for an added advantage. Take the example of China, Japan, Russia and all of Europe, everyone is more comfortable in using his or her own language. There is no culture in these countries, where speaking English makes you superior to others. They promote their own language and in every capacity inculcate the use of their own language. People learn English in non native English speaking countries just for the added advantage that might help them in their professions — that's all.

In India, regional languages are inferior to English. Parents who can't speak English fluently dreams of their child of speaking English fluently. Children can read and write more efficiently in English than in their own regional language. I have been brought up in a Hindi speaking household yet I am more comfortable reading and writing in English. I have to strain a lot while reading Hindi texts and keep utmost focus while writing in Hindi. There is a similar experience faced by my generation. My school and college focus on English; I was told by my parents and popular culture, that English would increase my social currency. In India if you are a young college grad and speak in English, you will be deemed superior to a more mature educated person who just can't speak in English as well as you; and this really bothers me. While India is teaching its citizens that English is superior, we are eroding the essence of one's language. If English is beautiful in construct than so is every other majorly spoken regional language. I get this sentiment that English bridges gap in a multi-diverse country like ours — but it cut both ways. The people in India are conditioned to believe that anyone speaking in English is far superior to the ones speaking in their own regional language. One thing that I can't wrap my head around is when two Indians — let's say knows Hindi as well as English but would choose to converse in English solely? I get the reason behind two people with different mother tongues conversing in a language that they both know. When people who know their own regional language very well, converse in English as their modus operandi, then you can make out that it is all about superiority and social status. These people want to be seen in speaking in English, and feel an inherent reward of conversing in a language that they find more superior than their mother tongues. For me, I converse in English with those people whom I can't converse in my mother tongue Hindi; for me English is to be spoken when required and is mandatory. I am writing all of this in English, because like many young educated Indians, we are made comfortable solely in reading and writing in English; well I am comfortable in speaking Hindi and but I am not at all reading or writing it. This colonial hangover makes me sad and when young people like me see English as their natural language of reading or writing — it feels that the Britishers left their mark so deeply that it might stay perpetually. In India, this feeling of being able to speak English has effectively cleaved the modern society. The people who are unable to comprehend the language or not given education in this language — find themselves in an inferior pool of society. Being able to speak English — is considered as something of a miracle in India — it gives an illusion of superiority.

I have seen and often felt in urban areas — the competition amongst parents for their child to speak fluent English — just to show them off or feel superior. It's a language for god's sake — not your superiority card. In India, if you go to the rural side and show your English skills — you would effectively establish the superior nature — and would find the rural people calling 'babu' and all. Biases in India is done by the colour of your skin, how well you speak English, religion, caste, occupation and the list goes on.

When Profession decides
your Social Worth!

One of the most appalling things that I find is the lack of empathy in India. When we compare ourselves with a modern western country, we talk about how their streets are so clean or how systematically everything functions. Now, when we look at our country and theirs, the difference that cuts across is the fact that people there have more empathy towards other citizens of their country. People treat each other with the respect that they expect from others and that is what basic civic sense and decorum demands. In India people treat people poorly; people treat people based on their societal hierarchy. Any person that comes in the bracket of manual labour like mason, plumber, electrician, carpenter and house servant will be ranked in the lowest level in the society. So any middle-class citizen who has a white collar job can treat them like second-class citizen in their own country. It is so common and casual in India that any form of person involved in such profession would be deemed so low that they wouldn't be permitted to sit on the same sofa as the one who is enjoying their services. When you divide a society on the basis of race, caste and profession, you can't have a society of equal measures. The western society has its own flaws and tension amongst races but it doesn't really pit profession against each other. A waiter or a plumber in America is a well-respected citizen who isn't treated as second-class citizen, the world doesn't tell the engineers, doctors et al that you are somehow superior but in India that is what it is. The country treats its people based on their incomes – if you are poor, then you will be treated badly, won't have access to the same education, rights, respect, living standards as compared to the ones who are in the middle bracket of the economic situation.

We are not talking about the rich – this section has always been the one to live a lifestyle that is glorious – and is more or less the same in every part of the world – having influence over the power and political concentration of a country. I am talking about the disparity amongst the poor and the middle class – the difference between a working class and the middle class. In India the working class are the people that have effectively considered as servants for the ever so growing middle class – the engineers, the doctors et al who are effectively employed by the rich. Now in this chaos of social order, we have the caste hierarchy amongst the already poor working class. Even amongst the drivers and the domestic help, the treatment is varied upon their castes. If a driver is of upper caste, then he (I am referring to a man because in India concept of a female driver are more or less non- existent) will be treated a tad bit better – given better food by his employer – allowed to sit on a sofa time to time – and shown a decent amount of respect that shouldn't be such a rarity.

In the minds of the middle class, it has been inculcated so deeply that a lower caste working class man or a woman is their servant and they will be treated as lowly as they could be. They will be given separate utensils to eat and drink; they would sit on the cold floors while we sit on the upholstered sofas and give them orders; the society would assume that they are dirty, filthy and lowly people who should be grateful that they are being employed at all. People would shamelessly boast that what a charitable person they are – giving the leftovers to their servants – clothes to their children which are discarded by their own children; they are treated as second-class citizen in their own country and presented as a form of charity that has been meted out to them. Then you ask why they are the criminals? Why they live in such poor conditions? Why are they so greedy? Why are they so ugly? Why there is so much of them? Why are they so poor? Why can't they just educate themselves and be like us?

We ask these questions and debate on it while we sip on our cocktails and bitch with other people of our own economic standings. We are no better than anyone and we won't be unless we give each profession the respect it deserves and the respect each person deserves. The false societal order has already corroded the country and is doing so presently; the working class is cleaved effectively by the politicians for their own gains who just wants their secured vote banks built on the foundation of caste politics and false promises. Politics only comes to sway people that one day their lives would be better if they vote in power the politicians with the sweetest tongue; the consciousness of the people should be appealed rather than their poverty and suffering to be toyed with just get some votes. Bribing them with luxuries that are only extended until the D-day of the voting comes in isn't the solution but a better understanding and upliftment philosophy has to be put in place. Before educating these uneducated and filthy servants, let's educate these so-called educated and clean hypocrites to understand how a better society can be carved if we treat people they we want ourselves to be treated by them.

The Indian Arranged Marriage Network

The Indian arranged marriage network is a combination of UN level diplomacy, high order social contacts and a reliable and society-approved way of helping your children get laid. People in other countries don't really get this and frankly speaking even I don't really get the logic behind this. The country where interaction between a man and a woman is largely a taboo has failed to grasp the very basic concept of dating or being in a relationship. For the majority of people in India — a man and a woman can be romantically involved only after they tie the knot. I am not saying that people don't date in India — they do but it is done either in secrecy or with the adherence to the conditions laid out by the respective parents. The country in terms of accepting that a man or a woman can choose their own partners is very rare; if their children are dating — then it's bad because they will lose focus on their studies or worse it is not what Indian culture permits.

Now, when the children are not encouraged to date or find their own partners — it has been from years been the responsibilities of parents to find their children — a wife or a husband. For a man, the marriageable age is flexible but generally it can be stretched as far as thirty years (though men's age is overshadowed by the incomes he is raking in); for women, after the age of twenty five — parents and relatives go in a frenzy and starts looking for prospective groom left, right and center. A girl unmarried after twenty-five is seen as a huge grievance; a girl unmarried after thirty is seen as a bad character and sadly becomes a topic of discussion in gossip circles.

Now, let's come to Indian men, they are expected to study well, bag a good package in a multinational and then after when they are settled — they would be paraded like a prized pony to attract the offers from prospective bride's parents. In India, it is not about the looks, personality, nature, humility, talent or any other feature that define a good personality that ideally should be a matter of choice for the bride or bride's parents but rather the family background and the groom's bank balance. Majority of Indian boys aren't expected to be sensitive or even caring, they are told to earn well and they can get a beautiful bride. In India, parents of a boy have a superiority complex (again this complex isn't based on merit but rather pure luck of conceiving a boy) while the bride's parents have inferiority complex forced upon them by the society. Maybe the girl is highly educated, holds a very good job and is a genuinely nice human being, but that doesn't matter, what matters is that she is fair and doesn't have any facial abnormalities as opposed to the groom whose looks aren't really the numero uno concern because he has been pumped by the society and his parents that he is the show pony because he works in a multinational company and earns a six-digit paycheck every month. BOOM!

One more thing that contributes here — is the lack of inter-gender interaction at grass root levels. To be honest, girls are only seen in India to just provide companionship to a man; the society here isn't familiar with the concept of a deep friendship or colleague interaction among the genders; the society only sees either the sexual involvement or romantic one. Girls and boys denied interactions from an early age, gets side barred into interaction with one gender only. A healthy society cannot function if both halves of gender are oblivious of inter-gender interactions. Now such fundamental anomalies have repercussions — this can be seen in the laughable patriarchal nature of the country. That's why men of India have different gender roles as compared to women of India. Again, this type of issue is not generalising but rather a majority trend in India. So, when you have boys and girls interact with their own respective gender from the start — you get problems of confused sexual urges. As the famous psychologist Maslow put sex as one of the basic needs with the likes of food, water and shelter; we Indians have seen sex as something that is taboo.

Sex in India is encouraged after marriage — it's not age restricted but rather marriage restricted. Now let's talk about the weirdest part of the arranged marriage network — the girl is expected to be a virgin while the boy doesn't necessarily need to oblige with this condition. The weird interlinking of purity of girls according to various religions is thrust here; men are men, so if they had sexual relations before marriage, it doesn't really matter but for a girl it is a sign of impurity, bad character and a red flag in arranged marriage network. In the urban sphere, where boys and girls tend to date and quite naturally have healthy sexual relations is to be of secrecy for girls while the boy can quite honestly boast about it because it wouldn't dent their reputation in the arranged marriage network. The first core value that guides the arranged marriage circle is hypocrisy and sexism that is accepted by the nation as a whole.

Is Dowry in India, a mere gift exchanging custom?

Now India is no stranger to customs that defies logic and sense; we adorn practices that are rudimentary, forcefully impose archaic laws and rules that have lost touch with the modern liberal society. One such shining example of this is 'Dowry', a practice that on paper is illegal and damnable but in reality is a reality and that too a very casual reality. That's the thing with India we take things that need to be dealt with seriously very casually and what needs to be taken casually very seriously.

Dowry is basically a demand put in by the groom's parents from the bride's; the demand is in the form of straight-up cash (it's like you are buying a husband for your daughter), gifts that include a brand-new motor vehicle or electronic items such as fridges, television, air conditioners etc. What is fascinating here is that this practice cuts all demographics; this weird practice that I personally unable to wrap my head around is common all across the lands of this country (with very few places as exceptions) and is common amongst the poor of the hut and the rich of the mansion. This belief that a groom's family is doing a favour to the bride's family of taking the responsibility of their daughter is very unusual to wrap your heads around. So, first this puts the man in a position of power, where he is the one who is superior and is capable of taking care of him and his wife; a woman is placed in a weaker position where she is handed off to tend to the needs of her husband and should be ever so grateful that he is providing for her. This is what dowry means in my logical sense, boy's parents first find a girl that would fulfill the sexual needs of their son as well as can be the caretaker of the house and the vessel to churn out babies to further the name of their lineage. I know I might have gotten harsh here; yes, I know all marriages don't have women in the weaker position of power but I am talking about an overwhelming majority where marriages are as similar as some sort of shady business deal. The girl's parents always considered lower in hierarchy compared to a boy's parents; this is hierarchy is decided on the ability to conceive a male baby as opposed to a female baby. The bride's parents biggest worry is to marry off their daughter and this burden has fallen on them by the very capable ideologies that are deeply embedded in Indian societies. Let's get back to the topic at hand—dowry seemingly innocent is very dangerous on this innocent spectrum. There are some families that believe in the beautiful practice of torturing the girl that has been married to their family because the due dowry hasn't found their greedy palms and coffers; the practice makes poor indebted in loan and the rich fear for the growing greed of their soon to be in-laws. Dowry treats all equally, making both rich and the poor miserable. In my opinion any relationship that needs financial incentives to begin with is a big red flag and is certainly cannot be pegged as a match made in heaven and holier than thou marriage outlook.

Boys will be Boys

A prominent politician of North India once justified the rape of a woman by presenting an argument that meant 'Boys will be Boys'. This argument baffles me. In our country, rape cases have been in an increment each passing year; casual sexual harassment has become a normal affair and every small sexual perversion finds its way into normalisation. Young girls to mature women, each one of them has to make peace with this weird notion that if something bad happens to them — there will be fingers pointing at their character or they would be advised to keep silent. The societal attitude where the victim is blamed, speaks of many things in volume. The country has time again shown its insensitivity towards the victim of any such crimes. Moral authorities questions the size of a girl's dress and the reason to be out so late in the night; police tries to shift blame by questioning the consent of the victim; neighbours tend to gossip which assassinates the character of the victim; everyone is trying to normalise the crime and not see the underlying problem. The problem of sexually frustrated men of this country.

First of all, there is no justification for any form of sexual indiscretion. People need to first learn what consent and what proper sexual conduct is. Secondly, we as a society promote gender segregation, which has effectively created sexual frustration and isolation. If boys and girls interacted from the grass root levels, there wouldn't be a lack of inter-gender empathy and a better society comprising of both men and women, with much greater respect and dependence on each other. Thirdly, it's never right to blame the victim — whether the girl is in a burqa or in a mini skirt — improper sexual conduct is not acceptable in any case; stop defending a rapist because the girl wore small clothes; if one doesn't have control over one's genitals, please seek medical help, because improper sexual conduct has no excuses.

Please, never appropriate this 'boys will be boys' bullshit, because it doesn't hold its ground. It's stupid and it's humanising the dehumanising act of sexually crazed men. This problem of thinking that if a girl is out there at night, wearing small clothes is a written consent, then get your head straight and please review the mental faculties inside of you. In India, the gender interaction is a big problem that no one really addresses; in the name of Indian handbook of culture, tradition and morality, the interaction between the two genders is frowned upon. No one actually realises that this is creating a sexually-confused army of boys — they don't know how to appropriately interact with women; they are sexually frustrated and skewed; for them consent is merely a word that doesn't hold up to any concrete principle in their sexual vision. Sex is one of the basic needs of a human being and as long as we make it a taboo, polarise gender and not educated the young boys about appropriate sexual conduct, we won't be able to witness a declining trend in rape, sexual assault , stalking cases etc. How many Nirbhaya do we need to address this issue and acknowledge that no boys will be boys attitude needs to be eradicated completely?

Online Harassment and Trolls

The Internet is beautiful – you can basically access information that was just a few years ago seemed more than impossible to get your hands on; but these days internet turned into something else entirely. Yes, it's good to have people with wide variety of opinions to share their views on social media platforms but when this simple concept of voicing your opinions translates into online harassment and abuse, then something has gone wrong catastrophically.

The year is 2017 and I can say this with confidence that putting anything online be it a picture of yours to sharing a meme to a political or personal opinion has a much higher chance of garnering hate than any constructive feedback. I get it, that people have different opinions and viewpoints, but it doesn't give you a go-ahead to go out bash someone on a social media platform who presented views that don't align with yours.

Though trolling is a worldwide nuisance but let's make our sole focus on the type of trolling niche to our country. I believe that Internet has somehow become a breeding ground for hatred due to a very pivotal feature of anonymity. I think deep down there's hate in every one of us but there are some who have just tapped into this insane amount of hatred to such an extent that this hate has become ugly and damnable. The Internet lets you be a critic of everything around, even though you are out of depth on most of the things to be even critiquing about. This is quite extraordinary in theory, that you can actually let your opinion be heard but in the more practical scheme of things, it has become a valley of endless hatred and abuses. Twitter—a shining example of 140 characters limit hate where people with different political opinions treat their counterparts with ugly hostility to people who just abuse, threaten and monger fear on any opinion that is different from the one they have.

Now, trolls target sections that are the weakest and is not expected to give a fight like women, teenage girls and controversial celebrities. Women on the internet face online sexual harassment on a daily basis. As a man, it was really hard to understand the depth of this sexual harassment that women in India go through daily, but the type of messages women get on social media platform from complete strangers is staggering.

The messages that are blatant show of sexual harassment has become so casual in India that most women choose to ignore these messages and move on with their lives. There are some instances where brave women had come forward and brought light to such issues but this crusade only limits to an educated elite class in urban spheres, while women in small parts of India suffer various kinds of sexual harassment on a daily basis. Online sexual harassment has now become a very big issue for women on the Internet, yet still we don't really address it immediately. India has this lax attitude towards sexual harassment where boys will be boys and girls should cover their self wholly, so to avoid this. This solution didn't work in real life and even in a virtual life where not even putting display picture, you would still attract sexually depraved ignorant perverts to harass them. India has gained a very notorious reputation in this online world of sexual misdemeanour.

The problem again here is the way 'sex' and gender interaction has been treated in India. From grass root levels, we have been taught that boys and girls shouldn't be friends. Teenagers are frowned upon we have they develop feelings towards the other genders and even though when you become an adult interaction with a girl is considered a taboo in majority parts of the country; this is the case why men don't have a proper mental development where he can see that a woman is not something of different species but has the same emotions, aspirations and urges as he does. When you suppress basic interaction and not talk about the basic sexual urges of both young men and women, then things will fall out of place. Men with no understanding of healthy sexual behaviours would do what their sexual instinct demands them to do and this leads to a society like ours where men openly stare down women of any age out in public spheres; the society where sexual harassment has become so casual is a society that is crying for help yet somehow seeing and hearing the cries all around us, we keep our eyes shut and our lips sewn shut. Even schools and colleges, that should encourage an environment where both sexes learn to work and learn together are more interested in segregating them and issuing proper guidelines for gender interactions. If we alienate boys and girls and limit their interactions to their own gender, then we are encouraging a population that is ill-equipped to properly co-exist in a society which is evenly populated with both of these sexes.

Love in India only looks good on silver screen

To be a lover in India is encouraged and discouraged at the same time. The Indian hypocrisy would make people root for their favourite movie actor to romance the actress. Almost all the movies and television serials produced in India is about love and romance. So, why is the Indian society against love in real life? We can all collectively cheer for the lovers on screen but in real life we discourage our children to get romantically involved.

In India, from one's childhood, it's discouraged to interact with the children of opposite gender. This is largely prevalent in rural and small towns across India. In urban areas, time has changed the attitude a little and gender interactions are less restricted. But it would be ignorant to say that young dating culture is encouraged in India. The county which is deeply conservative and overly religious always sees dating and love marriages as something of western philosophy that is destroying Indian culture. In India, to be in love and dating someone has always been a hush-hush affair. Parents and relatives need to be kept unaware of such knowledge. In India, families don't take kindly to their children dating or being in love. There can be severe repercussions for such acts. Though the punishments are more severe for girls compared to boys. From lectures to beatings to house arrest, the Indian societal control on love is quite menacing. If by any chance, your family doesn't mind that you are dating, then there are the moral police that might teach you a lesson. Various moral police that tells what one should wear, eat and do, are on a hunt to teach couples in India a lesson. On Valentine's day, such moral policing groups are in their most proactive mode and often resort to violent means. One more thing that is quite an Indian problem is the phenomenon of honour killing. Families kill their children in cold blood, if they besmirch the honour of the family by marrying or dating someone of their own choice and not approved by the family. Honour killing is the least honourable thing I have heard of but in India people are so opposed to love that they resort to cold-blooded murder. The country that is deeply divided by caste system and opposed to gender interaction, has made its young population to hide their love and desires. Arranged marriages are encouraged and love marriages are discouraged almost vehemently. Families in India would marry their children only to their niche castes, religion and socio-economic groups. Maybe for boys, the rules are a little relaxed but for girls it is quite regressive and strict.

Couples in India date in secrecy; often marry each other in secrecy. The society where love is celebrated on screen and despised in real life is a society that is hypocritical and messed up.

Feminism, Misandry and Patriarchy

It's the modern age where it is quite normal to believe that there isn't a superior gender. Though India can be seen as a patriarchal society at large, in recent years and especially in urban spheres, women are getting opportunities that they found themselves deprived of in olden days. The country which is deeply embroidered in religious values and ancient cultural practices had created separate roles for both men and women. Feminism in any third world country is different from a developed nation because western societies have always been years ahead in gender equality. The country still faces sex ratio inequality amongst boys and girls, and this can be accounted by the heinous practice of aborting a girl foetus. In rural India, girls are never given the privilege of education and at an early age married off. Though urban spheres as well as second-tier cities have grown in liberal values to educate and give equal rights to the girl child. The generation X of our country have been raised in patriarchy that the new generation Y or the millennials in India have learnt to see women in their families adopting different duties than the men. Indian society works on this idea that the boy of the family is the future scion of bloodline while a girl is some other family's asset. It's not correct to say that every family has this value system but it is correct to say that majority agrees with this. Working women are often considered as uninterested mothers; this sexist mindset dictates that after childbirth — a mother shouldn't work. Indian society makes women fight to make their own career — due to sexism and patriarchal think tank that had been placed in the system of ages old. Though the modern age has shown us icon amongst women that excel at sports, show business, educational professions and many others. But one thing is common amongst these icons is that they all have faced resistance in their making some way or the other. In India you also get rewarded for being a woman of independent and strong nature but on the other hand gets chided and mocked as well. Though it's a time where global exposure is at all time high and women across the country are breaking away from rigorous patriarchal structure, but still the struggle is there and it is real. If an Indian woman is confident, outspoken and dresses as per will, then she is deemed as arrogant, pompous and suggestive; if a woman is homely, shy and obeys the will of elders, then she is deemed as *sanskari*, pious and housewife material. The fear from confident and independent women is prevalent; one more thing that scares a man is the inability of proper gender interaction. We, Indians lack inter-gender interaction, because from the lowest level of schooling, boys and girls are taught to not interact with each other because it is not deemed proper in Indian society. The teenage years that are pivotal for two sexes to exchange gender nuances is often missing amongst the boys and the girls. The first touch and interaction of woman experienced by a man is generally during a marriage that is arranged by the respective groom and bride's parents. Such a society where men and women don't know how to platonically interact results in sexual frustration and in turn results in sexual misdemeanours. Every woman in India — from a ruralite to an urban dweller — they have faced sexual harassment in one way or the other. The continuous stare at public places and groping incidents at a crowded public transport is way too common for women in India. The normalisation has reached such a height that 'boys will be boys' are often said as consolation. Our boys need to be taught about proper conduct rather than normalising such sexual misdemeanours.

Now, let's move on from feminism to misandry. There is a double-edged sword and it cuts both ways. Men in India often face a gross generalisation and this is due to overwhelming sexual perverts roaming in the country. It's ignorant to say that there aren't perverts out there but it's more ignorant to say that all men are perverts. Misandry is there and is rarely talked about. Just like the global third wave feminism is on the rise, so is the misandry that it brings with itself on the table. If I am pro woman, then I am also pro man. If I can acknowledge women's problems, then I also want to acknowledge men's issues. In India, a woman can destroy a man's life by accusing him of sexual harassment or assault; the justice system heavily tilts in favour of women and even if it is established that the accusations were falsely made or had no basis — reputation of that man gets shredded into pieces. I have already talked about the sad customs of dowry, how women suffer from such a tradition but let's look at the fake dowry cases that are fabricated to frame an innocent man and his family to extract money and allowances. There is a notorious record of women falsely accusing men of asking for dowry or exaggerated domestic abuse claims. Though in lieu of feminism, liberalism and progressivism, women's rights should be championed, but what about men? It is clear that the world today is recognising the need for woman empowerment but it is also ignoring the rights and injustice suffered by innocent well-meaning men. If I am against patriarchy, chauvinism and archaic customs that targets women, then I am also against botched up feminism, misinterpretation of women's rights and generalising men into a circle of generalisation. In India, if we want society to prosper, then patriarchal customs as well as misplaced third wave feminism should all be frowned upon, and men and women out of mutual respect appreciate each other's struggles, strengths and importance.

The Godmen Epidemic

I am constantly boggled by this phenomenon: people in their most vulnerable state discards all kind of rationality and look for some form of miracle. From petty issues of disputes amongst family to that of health problems, people flock to respective branches of their religions. In India, when you go to any government department, you would experience roadblocks after roadblocks of inept government officials and bureaucracy; this is due to lack of management skills, ineptness of government employees and straight up corruption; if you want your work to be done in an efficient manner, you seek a middlemen, who will charge you certain fee for his services and eventually your work will be done. Similarly, people in India can seek their gods through temples et al, but as in our national consciousness, we have this habit of getting our work through the hands of middlemen; the middlemen being the self-proclaimed godman or the priests in a temple.

You are unable to secure that desired promotion in your job or not able to find a suitable suitor for your daughter or unable to build that house that you always wanted; fear not, these middlemen would charge you some fee and would claim to connect you to the network of your gods. Fear is the only reason religious exploitation exists. Fear is the only reason these middlemen can swim in all that cash flow. I have respect for a religious scholar — who speaks of spirituality and weighs in facts and effective logic — even helping people seek some calm in their life; I have no respect for these lowly priests, babas etc because they are straight up exploiting you. I am not religious, but I respect everyone's religious beliefs and affiliations; but what I don't understand is this insane fear that drive a religious believer to blindly follow these vile middlemen and politician, who doesn't give a damn about you and your religion, but are here to exploit you and spread hatred for others.

Let's look at some statistics. Currently, India has the largest population of illiterates in the world—amounting to 36% of the staggering population of 1.346 billion people which makes almost 287 million people who can't read or write. I brought attention to this specific number before I move on further with the topic at hand. The readers of this book would obviously fall into a population of men and women who are educated and intelligent enough to call a spade a spade; but the illiterate population of our country is not well equipped to think introspectively and constructively about many nuanced topics at hand— such as religion and politics. People ask what education does and why is it so important? Well it is important because it teaches the mass to think before they act and more importantly questions everything before jumping on a bandwagon.

Just look at any communal riot or mass hysteria, the foot soldiers in such kind of processions are the illiterate population of this country, who can be swayed so easily by religious and political factions. A well-read man wouldn't dare to go out become an arsonist by burning buses and destroying public property, when he gets offended; silent marches and peaceful staged protests may take precedence in more civil protest. Literacy is not only about no form of education but also covers the people who have been to primary or even secondary school but still haven't been educated—this section is not covered in the statistical figures. Thus the 287 million people are just a show figure but in ground reality, illiteracy has many different definitions and amount for more Indian population.

Now, let's talk about the self-proclaimed Godmen of this country. These men and women are clever and undoubtedly very crafty in their conduct. They know that their mass followers would be this illiterate population—which can be swayed easily by their honey laced tongues. Some of these bearded men wear cloaks of saffron, while some breaking stereotype of Indian sadhus and dons the modern attires of today. They would show magic tricks to excite these gullible audiences. They would also share miracle stories of men and women cured of deadly diseases, once they started following them. A mixture of godly magic (that is obviously staged) and a tool of fear of God often does the trick —making these simplehumans who are in no way special when compared to any of us, somehow gets elevated to a position of power and even revered as God or messiah of some kind. This power ropes in loyal followers which acts as an army if any opposition seeps in; this is seen by politicians as a large vote bank. Politicians seek the support of such Godmen and in turn, you scratch my back and I will scratch yours prevails. As we all know, that these Godmen can escape any form of crime with minimum repercussions (thanks to political overlords) because their endorsement means a large chunk of the leader's followers vote will fall in the politician's laps. Basically, these Godmen become invincible enjoying a status of power where law and order kneel before them. Hypocrites, one-word description for some of these Godmen that have multiple bases and an army of followers all around the country; this word is used because these leaders talk about the simple life of a 'sadhu', yet live in mansions and enjoy the luxuries beyond the imagination of their blind followers. Well, I need to hand one thing to these people, they have charmed the pants of millions of people. You need to have confidence, skill and some sort of brains to be able to make your own foothold in a country that is divided by many religions and beliefs.

In a nutshell, fear, illiteracy and magical realism have created an epidemic in this country where people blindly follows fools dressed in showman costumes to earn enough money to become insanely rich, gain ungodly powers and political influence. If this isn't a proof of that there is an epidemic of rise of such buffoons in our country, then what is?

I think we really need to address this untoward epidemic until a point is reached that it goes out of hand. The solution that is necessary is education and awareness; we need to eradicate this weird fear that ignorance carries with it, that often plagues the rural population of our country that have been deprived of critical thinking and put their blind faith in the hands of these 'babas' and 'Godmen', who just seek to exploit the fear the population harbours. Sometimes, these men and women follow these Godmen because they somehow feel isolated by the mainstream society; they may be segregated in terms of the caste system that treats them lowly or even the urban lifestyle that they can't associate themselves with. In these Godmen, they find someone who understands them or cares about them; the community of followers begins to feel accepting as compared to the urban masses and politicians who leave them high and dry. When we look for the rise of such Godmen, the main reason apart from education is also the caste system and ignorance of rural areas by mainstream media and politicians. We live in cities, and have niche communities around us, and our voices are constantly heard by the world; when you look at these rural areas, people are suffering, they don't have access to basic facilities like drinking water, toilets, hospitals et al. When the mainstream doesn't care about a sizeable population of our country, then they have to turn their heads and look for a messiah that can provide them comfort and strength. Enters Godmen to save them all.

The Flailing Indian Machinery

Superiority complex of the Police, Bureaucrats and Elected Representatives

A country is democratic in its truest sense when the elected representatives and the security forces don't look down on the common folks but rather engage with them eye to eye. Postcolonial India suffers from the superiority of anything related to government. Public servants like the police forces, elected politicians and even the Prime Minister of India act and behaves as if they are above the law and the democracy. At the ground level, a normal citizen is afraid to engage with a policeman and seeking the local elected representative is more or less an elusive dream. Police in India has such a bad reputation, that any Indian citizen would feel anxious rather safe and secure in their presence. Again there are always exceptional men and women in the police force but their name is squandered by the overwhelming numbers of bad apples. Police in India is inept, lazy and corrupt. They have a very bad track record in civil interaction with common folks; they are known take bribe to do their basic police duty; they are at the disposal of politicians and powerful men rather than the common citizens.

In developed countries, when a citizen sees a police officer — they feel secure and safe; in our country, a police officer means bribe or unnecessary hassle. Police in India is known to be insensitive to the plight of people and uninterested in solving crimes. In big cities, there might be times, where police flex their muscle in the pressure of media and the public but small towns and villages experience an utter disregard for justice. Police in India is corrupt and the politicians know that; in India rather than education or policy-making skills of a person qualifies him/her in politics but rather the money, backing and criminal record. Politicians and big criminals sometimes appear to be above the police; the police acts high and mighty in front of a common folk but low and pandering in front of the goons.

Elected politicians more or less have criminal records, black money and ego that makes them sit on a throne of their own inflated pedestal. The common working class and the middle-class are subservient to them; the upper middle-class has to pay for the services of police and politicians; the rich bankroll them and use them in their own accord. Anyone in India, who is associated with government and is in a position of power feels superior to the common folks. The term 'public servants' falls on deaf ears. In papers, everyone is equal in the eye of the law and the constitution but ground reality is far from the idealistic principles.

We are not subjects of a Monarch

Winston Churchill raised his doubts about Indian freedom and success; he pointed out that Indians will devour itself and the democracy should be played in the hands of educated classes. To counter such thinking, our educated and political veterans drafted the constitution is such a way that it provided universal adult suffrage as well as fundamental rights for an individual to be free in this country. The architect of the constitution, B R Ambedkar kept in mind that people of India are not to be treated as subjects but as free citizens of democratic India.

The lawmakers and the law enforcers have this notorious habit of curtailing this freedom and reducing the uneducated classes as mere subjects. Being in a high post of political office or even a police force doesn't change the fact that you are a servant of the public; the VIP culture and the pompous attitude of the power sets India to the discourse of a monarchy. The educated classes are argumentative, aware of their rights and don't easily succumb to ostentatious demands, but the uneducated classes lack all of these. In India, democracy is only understood and enjoyed by a certain section of the country, while the farmers and rural population are treated as 'praja' in a monarchical setup. This habit of the politicians or anyone in having power in the government of superiority and habit of being above the law and constitution really hampers the idea of democracy. When politicians start deciding what you can eat — you can see autocratic attitude; when the police extort money or consider itself above the law — then it's anti-democratic; when you see leaders leading the people without the discourse of free dialogue — then its dictatorial attitude.

The constitution of India proved one thing — that our leaders back then rightly assessed the situation and gave immense freedom to its citizen. While national level to state-level leaders are considering themselves as monarch, but in reality they are on a payroll of the common folks. The body of the judiciary is still intact and is efficient in some way to call out the undemocratic nature of the government time to time. The country is not a communist regime or a fascist one, but a democracy where people's voice should be heard. If the power is given to you by this praja, then it can be snatched away from you. Treat every citizen in India with the respect that they deserve — from an uneducated rural farmer to an educated IT professional — all are India's citizens and rightly have their say in the biggest democracy of the world.

Nepotism in India is an age-old concept:

From smallest of professions to the biggest of them all — nepotism runs deep in Indian society. I have nothing against nepotism — if one generation worked hard — then it's alright for generations to follow to reap its benefits. But in India nepotism takes a very peculiar form. Sometimes it elevates mediocrity and ignores excellence.

The biggest example where nepotism works is either in political parties shifting power in the hands of one particular party; similarly if someone is holding a government office in any capacity, then he/she would try by any means possible to land a similar job for their family members. Nepotism run is every socioeconomic level of this country — from a small shopkeeper to a large business entity. The assets of a business would circulate within a family. A doctor's son would try to get a medical degree and join the family line of work; similarly suit for any other profession. In India it's either joining the family business or starting from scratch.

A big debate surface recently — nepotism in Bollywood. Obviously there is nepotism in Bollywood and in fact in any film industry across India. When we make young generation of Bollywood family apologies and feel guilty, then we should look inside our conscience and apologise to the world as well. Majority of Indians are a product of nepotism. From inheriting small family shop to a business venture, the country is no newcomer to the practice of nepotism.

In our country, there is always a strong emphasis laid on *khoon ka rishta* (blood relation), that control should run inside a close-knit circle. Such an attitude creates halts and problems.

Political families fighting over successor in a long line of the family; brothers and sisters fighting for that piece of pie out of the family will. Nepotism in some way paves the way for an easier life for young generation but can also be a messy affair.

Now, nepotism comes across as a problem, when by hook and crook it promotes family despite clear demerits and lack of capability. Many talented souls get overlooked because of prevalent nepotism. A young talented actor would eventually lose to a film producer's kid; a social worker with political ambition would always find himself/herself down the pecking order of dynasty political practices; jobs are favoured in professional sectors to family members. Talent matters but in India blood trumps all; mediocrity is never a factor but moving the name of a family is what motivates Indian minds.

The Mediocrity and Inefficiency of Our Government

The government is inept, lazy and corrupt — it has been the attitude and the norm since the country gained independence. Anything associated with the government automatically means mediocrity and tardiness. Ask any Indian about their experiences with any government official or babu, policemen or *thulla* or any other government official— the overwhelming majority will tell about their experiences that would fall on the negative spectrum.

The epitome of laziness and inefficiencies are the babus sitting behind the desk of millions of government offices across the country. Any errand that requires an Indian to pay a visit to a government office is always considered as a work of great pain and wait; even though the errand is as good as of few minutes but a government official's laziness would stretch it to a task of gargantuan proportion. When you visit an RTO office for getting your driving licence — you can wait for hours in the line outside — or like many middle-class folks — contact a middleman who would get you ahead of the line and get your errand be done in a matter of minutes. The sum you owe the middleman would be distributed to the *babu* as well. It is the trend to make a quick buck here and there — and for you it is easy to shell a few bucks, then stand in line for the whole day for an errand that should require less time. That's the way it operates — if you are moderately wealthy, then you can hire the services of countless middlemen hovering around government entities and get your work done. And it is a common knowledge that in India, you can get your driving licence made without actually knowing how to drive a car (this is pretty self-explanatory when you see the beautiful chaos of traffic in the country).

Basically, it has seeped into Indian consciousness that to get work done, you need to either bribe the *babu* or get a middleman who knows the proper ins and outs of a government office to get your work done. This model of cutting line getting work done is prevalent in our temples as well — if you have money to shell and want to avail services of your favourite God without the inconvenience of standing in a huge queue — then you can get express darshan, VIP darshan or the elite VVIP darshan. Basically be it a government errand or a religious one — all you need is a little cash flow to get yourself pushed ahead of the line. I have already talked a lot about the logic being absent in India — when it comes to religion — when people pay for their convenience to pray to their favourite Gods — then it should be understood that there is something wrong with how the religion is being operated and treated.

Let's get back to the lazy babus — where on paper earns a very moderate salary but in reality takes home a handsome salary. In India, if you do your work with dedication and with efficiency, you would become a villain overnight. People and the system don't expect you to work fairly — they want you to be corrupt. People like me on the surface would say that police and government official should be honest and not corrupt — but to be honest — people like me — the urban middle class are the utmost beneficiaries of this skewed system. Poor people don't get the luxury of front row RTO , passport office etc services through bribery; poor people don't get to bribe traffic policeman when infringing a traffic law — it is inconvenient for us to get a fine slip and pay the fine through the official way — for us to stick a green note for the policeman is much easier. The thing is everyone in the system is corrupt — because this country promotes mediocrity, dishonesty and skewed morals. When the middle classes and the rich want all the facility in the world without actually waiting, then the society would obviously bend the rules for their convenience — as per the poor people they wait in line — while people like us shell some bucks and cut lines.

Corruption and India

Corruption in India is basically a headless monster; everyone is aware of the evil but no one knows whom to slay. Whenever a problem starts from a lower level, then it has been embedded in so deep that it almost feels impossible to remove it. Every country in the world has this kind of deep-rooted problem which they find almost impossible to eradicate completely. For India, if I have to point out one problem that plagues the poor as well as the rich and uneducated as well as the educated, then it has to be corruption. In India corruption is both visible and not visible at the same time. The visible corruption is that makes the headlines — where scams worth of crores has been done — big names have come into the limelight — all of this is done either by the lieu of political vendetta or just to throw dirt on opponents during a dirty election fight; whenever a new scam surfaces, a debate about corruption, black money and government comes into forefront. Its lifespan is quite short and the whole hullabaloo dies down within few weeks; no one cares anymore about the accused and the whole scandal. Indian anger is as good as the media circus around news coverage; people move on with their lives and goes back to the daily grind of Indian life. The visible corruption is good for newshour debates, textbook references and college debates. It's visible because, it has been designed to be made visible. There are instances where corruption scandals are unearthed by hard-working journalist who meets with a dire fate. So any visible corruption scandal is either politically motivated or just the hard work of some journalist. (chiefly the former ones presides).

The invisible corruption or rather I would like to call it the normalised corruption. This sort of corruption is invented, innovated and put into regular habit by the public themselves.

This is done because the proper way of doing anything (that is government affiliated) is taxing and consume time, resources and efforts. One of the most common examples is bribing a police officer; if you jumped a red light and stopped by a policeman (rarely happens; majority of people in India doesn't really care about red lights), then you have two choices: either get a fine where you have to go to a local court and pay it or just pay the policeman, a crisp note of a rupee. People would actually take the first choice, but everyone in India knows the condition of our courthouses and how this can consume a whole day or maybe a couple of days or even weeks; so the easier way out is always chosen. Now, in India, from the judiciary to the lawmakers, the majority is seen as inefficient, unreliable and to be avoided at all cost, if you don't want any hassle. Now, the government employees or any form of government affiliation means that if you want your work to be completed in an efficient manner, then bribing is mandatory. For instance, if you want to get your driving license made, then in order to get it done swiftly and efficiently, you gotta bribe the clerk and the passing officer; then when after a while the postman from the government postal services knocks at your door — you have to grease his palms as well; similarly when you get your passport made and the police comes for mandatory identification, you have to grease his palms too; these courtesy bribes are also a norm in our country, because if anyone in government is not bribed, then you can expect your almost completed government work to be put on hold. Almost anywhere in India, wherever you see a government office, and you'll go in there with an idea of honesty and good citizenship, then prepare for an arduous and torturous assault of government employee's notorious laziness, inefficiency and peculiar attitude.

Now let's visit the more serious: invisible corruption. I am talking about black money. Basically it's the assets that you have not shown on papers to avoid taxation, well that's the basic gist of it. Now, in India it is reported that at about 1% of the population pays their taxes. What does it say? That the overwhelming people in India have black money from very small amounts to that of huge hordes. From a common man to a big shot celebrity to a politician to a billionaire, all somehow have black money. Every government that ruled the centre since independence saw its politician amass wealth and thus no one really cared about combatting black money. Though in the winter of November 2016, PM of India declared currency of denominations 500 and 1000 as null and void; this was done to combat black money. Anyway a year later, due to severe lack of planning and the usual inefficiency of government, we saw demonetisation create more of a problem than a solution. The new 2000 denomination note feels to make matter much easier for black money hoarder now; though despite these cons, one thing I that at least after all these years, centre decided to act on the black money issue that plagues our country. To be honest, the implementation was bad, the effects are rather long-term and in short terms it overstressed the economy and created public distress. Just like every corruption crusade, the fight against black money ceased to exist. Such a public momentum was gathered during the anti-corruption movement during the year 2011. Anna Hazare and Arvind Kejriwal, the faces of this movement saw a popular uprising and enjoyed heavy public support to get Lokpal Bill passed. The bill was aimed to check corruption at every level it the government bureaucracy; the centre at that time responded but the public backed movement grew leaps and bounds, but to see all was a short live agitation. When I saw this popular uprising about six years ago, I saw the cunning Kejriwal, who shot to fame, formed a political party, became the Chief Minister of Delhi, sidelined Anna Hazare and the anti-corruption stance. Eventually he became the cog in the dull, broken down and dilapidated political machinery. Similarly the 2016 demonetisation can prove to be borne out of ulterior motives and can in the coming years feel like the past anti-corruption crusades.

Again the solution to make India corruption free will feel vague. In a society, where a child sees his parents bribing other people as something quite common — then a parent's counsel to not exercise any form of corruption would feel hypocritical. A system where the education is meted to just a handful of society, and there too just scoring marks and getting into an engineering or medical college is the aim and no need for a lesson in societal uprightness, talks of corruption free India will feel stupid and vague. A system and a society that thrives on corruption to get things moving and the sizeable portion of earning is through everyday corruption, then that society cannot be corruption free overnight or by some token slogans, speeches and a few Bollywood movies on such issues. The problem is deeply-rooted and the only solution is by educating from the lowest level about what corruption is and why it is not ideal for our country; at least the future generation will be a little better off than the past and the present Indian generation who all have been born and learnt to live amongst the corruption of every day.

From a small shopkeeper to a big tycoon; from a slum dweller to a resident of a posh flat; from a minimum wage worker to a high paid employee; from a civilian to a supreme court judge; everyone faces corruption, takes part in it and at some point encourages it. The modern Indian society has given up on its elected government, police department and the judiciary to resolve problems and let society function smoothly. That's why we have a parallel economy that stays afloat because of our contribution to the vicious cycle of corruption. Sometimes I feel corruption is good for our country, at least by bribing someone or evading taxes, you are subscribing to a life that is comfortable and much simpler than the rotten system of honesty. Gandhi's values and morals only uphold when speeches are made or when children are taught about Indian history; the society runs in its own vague terms, where everyone is a part of corruption because of the lack of reward from the society when you try to be a Gandhi or an honest man.

The Dying *'Nyaypalika'* of this Country

Audiences love courtroom dramas, they have all the recipe for complete entertainment and it also gives us closure in a sense that justice has been served. Lawyers arguing — trying to one-up each other — the obvious culprit and the victim is the one who is poor and begging for justice. Eventually in our movies, the judges act quickly and decisively, and eventually we see justice being meted out properly. If only this scenario was the ground reality of our justice system.

The country's record of pending cases in courts is the worse amongst the world. There are many reasons for this, but the numero uno reason that stands out is the dwindling number of judges appointed in the vast vacant posts. There are almost 2.8 crore cases that are pending in various courts across India and around 60,000 matters pending in Supreme Court.

The problem is not that people aren't coming in with new cases but the problem is very few are going out the justice inlet. Police, which is supposed to be the perfect instrument of law, order and justice machinery is often unruly, unprofessional, disrespectful and 60% of the time makes false or unmotivated arrests.

There are external matters such as few number of judges, less number of courts and the dilapidated infrastructure of the majority of the courts. The internal factors are the outright corrupt nature of all those involved in the matter of courts and the unsophisticated mechanism of conducting a trial. Cases may come and people wait for their much-awaited justice but all they can do is wait for the delayed justice. People who have been affected by crimes or grave injustice, can only aggravate their suffering further by first seeing the inefficiency of Police investigation (in most cases) and then to suffer the slow and arduous torture of the court proceedings that can take a lifetime. People pass away, but their cases remain alive in the dates of hearing that get pushed year after year. That's the ugliness of this all; the vilest thing an enemy can say to you is that I wish you get the misfortune of roaming around courts to get justice.

People have already lost their faith in the politicians; people have already faith on the police; people are now losing faith in the judiciary. The lost faith in the judiciary is the final nail in the coffin. There are many holistic ways to improve the judiciary system but in the case of India, it's most likely a dream for utopia.

Journalism and India

Journalism can never be silent: that is its greatest virtue and its greatest fault. It must speak, and speak immediately, while the echoes of wonder, the claims of triumph and the signs of horror are still in the air.

Henry Anatole Grunwald

So, journalism is a profession that is an essential part of democracy; the last time I checked, our country is dubbed as the world's largest democracy; then why the hell, journalists, who are the products of this democracy are the ones who are vulnerable and susceptible to the fringe elements of our society? Journalism is not a mouthpiece for political parties and their leaders; it talks about what is happening and if it is unable to find what's happening, it has fold to it's shirt and dig deep and find the truth that is deeply buried in dirt and shit.

It has become a trend for politicians and any other factions that get called out for their wrongdoings by an honest journalist to agitate in the vilest manner. Threats to one's and one's family's lives—a common affair for an honest journalist; on the other if a journalist indulges in sycophancy, then he/she gets its rewards from the overlords. These days, journalism is at war again. The war is of facts that they present. The facts are bitter but are of truth. Mainstream wants sugar-coated pills, which is provided through fake news, that is propaganda at best.

In India, a weird trend of making political leaders seem like an avatar or a demigod has been running for a while now. The people are made to believe that their leader is a god or a saint and for you to question his or her motive is a sin. Basically, cunning political advisors have taken its cue from religion where to question the morality is a sin in itself. This sin is committed by journalists; for which they get online threats to more menacing physical repercussions. In fact history hasn't been really kind to any form of dissent and the biggest example is that of the Indian agitation during the British Raj; though the difference was that it was considered dissent not anti-national behaviour because it was against a foreign rule but if you dissent against an Indian government, it is by decree sedition or anti-national behaviour.

Whistleblower's, journo's, social worker's and any concerned citizen's dissent would get suppressed by either the government, wealthy faction or criminal strongholds and the difference is that if the dissent is against the government, then it's sedition. Killing in the name of supposed nationalistic ideologies or straight up to hide the exposure of one's wrong deed is quite common in India. I feel, why on Earth these foolhardy men and women, try to fight against a system that is broken to its core; they are outnumbered by blind followers and men who can buy the system to use them as a shield against all their evils. Why on Earth do these people fight the system? They fight because their constitution has given them a right and this right is known as the right to freedom and speech.The country is not run by a dictator or any form of unelected form of government; to speak against the evil of the government and the criminal faction is the dissent that is needed and it is stemmed from the roots of the most nationalistic morales of all the freedom fighters and dissenters who fought for this democracy. To dissent is to be nationalistic and what is anti-national is the blatant abuse of government power and influence.

Are we a country of hurt sentiments?

Time and again, we face this question: Are we a nation of hurt sentiments and fragile sensibilities? Time and time, we prove that we somehow are; though on paper, we are a democracy and on the global stage, we boast of being the largest of all. When we claim that we are the largest democracy and then see our track records in proving that freedom of speech, expression and thoughts are limited to a certain sphere. There is a fine line between what is freedom of speech and what isn't. We easily throw terms like anti-national and sedition; while the hate speeches in the name of religion flow under the radar. The thing with freedom in our country is that it comes in certain clauses and conditions. Before we begin, let me just tell you that I know that our country is democratic and tolerant enough for me to even muster enough courage to criticise it; for those politicians, ignorant population and clearly trolls hiding in the dark corners of the internet who gets their feathers ruffled, when we criticise our country and start this weird promotion of Pakistan tourism — I want to say just one thing — I don't care about Pakistan, Saudi Arabia or any other god damn country with a bad reputation in freedom department; I am concerned with our country's well being and I look at successful countries that are developing morally and philosophically, due to the healthy criticism they have learned to take from their citizens.

The law pertaining to Indian freedom of speech and expressions are flimsy and laughable to say the least — they aren't concrete enough to rely on; while on the other hand, look at US' First Amendment — it gives an immense cushioning to its citizens and a great deal of freedom to its press. Even the US congress can't pass any bill or adopt a way to curtail such freedom. Look at the local level participation of US citizens

131

in their local government or societal issue; the freedom their press has; the audacity of comedians is such that they can openly mock any politicians; their outspoken nature, where a citizen is not afraid of being an icon of offence. The thing is: freedom of speech doesn't mean giving hate speeches, speaking racial slurs or outright sedition-mongers; such acts are of criminal nature and this doesn't come under the idea of free speech. But in India, anyone having an opinion away from the mainstream gets pushed into the sea of sedition or hate speech category, while the real culprits evade the limelight of hatred.

The country doesn't really rely on critical or individual thinking but rather what the mob is thinking at the moment; we are so impressionable as a country, that whenever a popular leader says let's take offence — with closed eyes, we take offence. Politicians and religious leaders benefit from such a volatile Indian mentality; politicians start taking offence to either entice their vote banks or score a political vendetta; religious leader do such things to promote their skewed religious propagandas — be it a bigoted Muslim Cleric or a Hindu fanatic Baba — they have army of followers that rely on what these godmen are gonna do. Now, the minority who questions such offence taking habits are the most vulnerable and prone to hatred of the mobs. Such population consists of journalists, news anchors, writers, songwriters, filmmakers, actors, painters, musicians, comedians etc. They face the ire or face the music when they become too liberal in their freedom of speech and expression practices.

Every country has a right to love, cherish and protect their history, religious practices and past traditions; but Indians are so overprotective that without thinking twice, if any conversation of critical nature comes about, we are ready to answer with fire and fury. Any movie made on historical events or contains any form of religious criticism or mentioning will be put under the public microscope. The creative right for a filmmaker to present his/her take on events of historical significance and religious outlines is fundamental; yet we as a country start taking offence. Its right to take offence, if the movie is genuinely hurting people and has undertones of racial or religious hatred, but our country doesn't care about all of this. We are just adamant about this fact that we need to please every single sensibility. Even a children's animated movie will offend someone somewhere — does it mean it should be banned? People are so sensitive to religion and history, that even a slight mention is provocative enough for a group of people to stand up and protest. The protesting is done in a vile manner: burning of effigies, death threats to the artists involved in the said controversial movie/song and sometimes serious physical harm to them as well. The politicians who are given this responsibility to maintain law and order, and provide moral counsel to these triggered sections, care more about not to upset these people who voted them to power; they are more concerned about their vote banks of the next elections rather than carrying out their duties. Various religious groups, unions or any section of the society who have taken offence makes life a living hell for these filmmakers and anyone associated with that film. The problem is that no one actually cares about what they are hurt about but they are hurt and offended because their neighbour is hurt and offended; individualistic introspection and seeing why they are offended is never considered. In India, our filmmakers stick to the same song and dance routine that doesn't touch upon religion, any real social issue, a critique of the government in power and historical events. As a nation, we rightly deserve the same processed garbage, because we scare away the good artist who wants to come out and do something that is of substance. The intellectual demise of leaders who call the shot promotes butthurt morons, who don't know about the deep significance of their own religion and a straight fact about historical events that they are hurt about.

There is a way to show your discontent, if you disagree with someone's work; by saying you don't like it and bringing out a constructive form of debating challenge in person or through social media. If you don't like a film — that's alright, you can review it badly and but by getting offended and start acting violently is something really undemocratic. Hey listen, it's alright if someone doesn't like the politician you admire; it's okay for someone to make a film that you don't approve of because if they have the right to produce a film, you have the right not to watch it; hey, if someone is criticising your religion, you can debate him/her and not prove him or her right by issuing death threats and being violent in response. If there is a comedian who tells a joke, that you don't agree to — then you can not applause and appreciate him/her because you have all the right not to find a particular comedian funny; similarly the comedians don't hold a card to adhere to everyone's sense of morality and offence mechanisms. India is a democracy — you can debate, speak, talk, joke, sing, dance etc about anything you like — but our reaction to this shouldn't be violent or hooliganistic public outrage but rather a silent protest, constructive debating and even social media ranting. Let's not make politicians act as if they are in an autocratic country and let's not make religious leader believe that they are some form of invincible forces; they are in public eye, they are bound to be the butt of jokes and will be the cartoon caricatures in the media. It's a democracy and not even a Prime Minister is above it or neither are you.

Left and right in Indian context

The argument as a whole, whether left wing or right wing politics is better suited to India is fairly pointless. The country has always been largely right wing in its conduct and never really leaned towards the left. If unfortunately, the country leaned left, it paved the way for the extreme left ideologies of communism. Creation of Naxalites and Maoists have spelled trouble for many states of our country and showing the vulnerability of extreme left politics. Now, let's talk about the extreme right politics that calls for Hindu state and call for anti-secular slogans; the extreme right wing wants religious intolerance and brings India back to ancient ways that disregard western corruption. Both extreme left and right are dangerous and propaganda for doom. The country has always been right winged in its demeanour; the liberal left was only limited to metropolitan cities and more specifically to the bounds of liberal colleges.

Now, the right ideology of this country looks for religion, patriotism and family values as the focal point. It accepts globalisation to the point of economic growth; it accepts western ways limited to sectors such as education, health, finance and technology. It disregards western aspects of morals and values, because they can corrupt the traditional Indian way of living. The right-wing politics always has a strong sense of patriotic attitude that sometimes can push towards a jingoistic viewpoint. They believe in heavy spending of military and also makes questioning the military as a grave form of disrespect. These are the basis of the right wing, and I respect such views because since the Indian freedom, it never really posed a threat to Indian secularism and free speech.

If we look at the liberal or the ideology of the left in a purely Indian sense, it's limited to the educated urban class. Left-liberals in active stance might seem like a dwindling minority, but the real number of such beliefs are of the silent majority. This is opposite to the case of America, where the silent majority, this time proved to be the right-wing conservative population. Left-liberals in India believe in secularism. Liberals believe in socialism more as opposed to capitalism. They want less disparity amongst poor and the rich. The heavy basis of liberalism is accepting the positives of foreign cultures and do away with some of the taxing ancient customs that are no longer relevant in modern society. Left-liberal believes in a more transparent role of the military, which can make any member of the military feel accountable for any wrongdoing rather than feeling untouchable because of army status. They believe in less censorship and freedom to express free speech via journalism, arts and cinema.

Both these ideologies are required for a society to function properly; though the mainstream politics is right winged, but that doesn't make people not wanting to adopt good liberal values. Similarly the right wing values of tradition and customs make a common feeling of nationhood and keep the roots of our culture intact. Now, we need both these beliefs to run in unison. But sadly the country always seem to either lean towards the extreme left or the right. As I earlier stated, the extreme left led to the Naxalite and Maoist problems; the extreme right leads to communal violence which raises question over the country's tolerant attitude, secular ideas and free speech ideals.

The extreme right factions are always the tools that right-wing politicians unleash to exert more muscle power; on the face value it's really bad to discriminate against the non-Hindu minorities but in silent conversations it is quite alright. False propaganda of portraying the minority Muslim as the ultimate threat to India has paved the way for the political uprising of Hindu extremism. The point here is that Islamic terrorism is condemnable and anyone promoting it is by default a criminal;

let the police, army and counter-terrorism departments do their jobs and not paint your next door Muslim neighbour as a potential terrorist. I do understand the fear against Islam and its quite clear that the core values of Islam are dangerous, misogynistic and not compatible with the functioning of modern society, but it doesn't mean that you would expect all Muslims to disregard their religion in a heartbeat. Even Hinduism and Christianity have their flaws, but as rational men and women, we choose not to accept them. To disregard one's religion is almost as stripping away your culture and core value system. Let me clarify this in a more simplistic fashion. If a young Muslim of modern India has been going to the Mosque from his childhood and celebrating Eid for all these years, then Islam for him is a way of communal gathering and a part of his culture. He has friends from all the religion and is fairly educated and has disregarded the jihadist and misogynistic teachings of Islam, but still wants to be a Muslim, because it's the reminder of his childhood, family values and the communal upbringing. There are Hindu prudes, who differentiate between people due to the caste system, promotes patriarchy and forces women of the household to submit and be deprived of many opportunities. So does a modern-day Hindu promote such ideology? Because some are corrupt in his religion, will he renounce his religion? Religion for a human being is about social gatherings, family values and childhood memories. Being a Muslim doesn't mean you are a jihadi terrorist; if you follow Islam in all its entirety, then there might be a problem and as equivalent to following ancient Hinduism, Christianity etc.

Extreme Right, Polarization and Indian constitution

The constitution of India clearly says that our country is a secular one — that gives every citizen a right to follow his/her religion. That's the beauty of this country — the big heart to embrace all religion and belief system. But when you are forcing your religion on others — it is a direct violation of the ethos of our sacred constitution. When Hindu nationalists and extreme right faction tries to impose their religion via favouritism of its followers and bias towards another belief system — then it is counter-intuitive to their jingoistic viewpoints; when you say that you are a *desh bhakt* — it clearly means that you embrace Indian constitution that doesn't differentiate between castes and religious beliefs. The Hindu extremism stems from a belief system of intolerance of other religions and counter-intuitive ideologies of patriotism that promotes patriarchal and archaic customs. Now, similarly other prominent minorities like Muslims and Sikhs have extreme right factions as well. It's not just that Hindu extreme right is a source of irrational and counter-intuitive ideologies; mainly all major religions in the world has the extreme right that are intolerant in their ideas.

The extreme right of the Islam has always been the catalyst for the rise of extreme right Hinduism; India also saw extreme right Sikh movement in pro-Khalistan movements; the globe around also see extreme right resurgence in either Christianity, Judaism, Buddhism etc. The majority of the population has always been tolerant and secular in conduct, but the extreme right of few has always been the source that is based on hatred and intolerance towards other religions. The Muslim extremism in India have created various terrorist factions involved in the mass killing of innocents; similarly the Hindu counterparts have also been involved in communal violence. There are many conclusive pieces of evidence that one act of hatred creates another act of hatred in retaliation. A sane Muslim or a Hindu, who believes in the Indian constitution's secular principles couldn't possibly endorse such instances. People in India have always shown acts of sympathy and love towards each other but hatred of some and the political motivation of polarising makes ordinary citizen more skeptical of their neighbours.

Now, the polarisation happens in media and politics — the biggest influencers for an ordinary citizen. Media based on religious bias either portrays exaggeration — from minorities being oppressed by the majority or majority is in threat of the excessive appeasement of the minorities. In common Indian experience — such claims are misrepresentations of Indian experiences. An Indian regardless of his/her religion faces similar challenges and rewards. The polarisation by media and politics is done to create clear-cut vote banks and divert Indian attention from clear-cut problems. Poverty plagues everyone — Hindu, Muslim, Sikh and every religious group in India; hunger is a human fallacy and malnutrition comes despite religious preferences; lack of sanitation causes diseases to a temple goer as well as a mosque-goer. The basic problems of India affect everyone — the country houses many religion and all are facing same rudimentary problems; the narrative sold by the media, politicians and extreme right factions are just to create a rift amongst secular country that has been modelled after colonial rule by revolutionaries, freedom fighters and Gandhian ideologies. The country has seen Sikhs, Hindus, Christians, Muslim and many other religious groups live as neighbours and dream of a secular India that will prosper. The elusive dream is being replaced by the religious intolerance of extreme right movements in every religious department and to succumb to it is anti-national and if you don't believe me, please visit the beautiful preamble of our country's constitution.

Epidemic of Fake News and
Political Trolls

Internet connectivity and the social media revolution brought technology, entertainment and education at every house in India. The Internet boom somehow changed the way we consumed news and formulated an opinion. In India, people get easily influenced and also has this habit of herd mentality. Social media sites like Facebook, YouTube and Whatsapp made Indians more involved in their politics and popular culture. Usually the urban dwellers were vocal voices and opinionated minds, but technology has made everyone an opinionated soul. Politicians quickly assessed the new ground reality — and hence begun the rise of fake news.

In India, people don't really care about the sources, facts and authenticity of anything but rather likes to believe whatever they are spoon fed. Doctored images, videos and articles reach the mobiles and computers of urban as well as rural Indians on a daily basis. False information and fake visual representation can spread like wildfire through WhatsApp forwards, Facebook and YouTube shares. Fake news of religious falsities aiming to provoke religious factions against each other or promoting a particular political party's agenda is on the rise. The new political jibes and religious hate war is fought by the Internet militia of trolls.

Fake news instigating hatred amongst religions have shown real-life cases of mob violence, vandalism and criminal activities. Fake news spreading false propaganda makes a political leader look like a saint and a genius, but in ground reality, the list of achievements and inspiring stories are all made up. Fake news in the name of religion are done to polarise communities; fake news glorifying politicians are done to win elections; fake news in the name of India's achievement fans fire to destructive jingoism. In totality, an epidemic of fake news is on the rise, and Indians are consuming it voraciously. When the world starts to feel unreal and the news we consume lacks facts and credibility, then it questions our own intellect and morality.

Images taken from somewhere, context put from somewhere and the newly made fake news that is served not only fans communal hatred but confirms our deep hidden bias; at the end, religious fanatics need a reason to slit each other's throat; politicians need scandals to throw dirt at each other; people need entertainment and that we can get from fake news.

People are consuming and spreading fake news; social media giants are okay with them; polarisation of opinions are creating more and more fake news. The world has seen the rise of leaders that spew pure lies; in India we are witnessing the era of lies; the post-truth world seems to boost the epidemic that is fake news.

Epilogue

Armchair activism, shedding jingoism and vision for India

Now, by writing this book, I am effectively fallen into the category of armchair activism. I have talked about, made fun of, seriously pinpointed and even provided logical reasons for the above-mentioned problems; that's armchair activism. Some would say — it is so easy to list out the problems; some might say that people like 'you' can only talk and won't bring about change that you want. At least, I am acknowledging the problems our country is facing; many young men and women are trying to bring this sort of discussions in mainstream debates — call it armchair activism — but it is at least something. As opposed to jingoism, where people don't even want to acknowledge that there is anything wrong in this country. If we let go of every form armchair activism — journalism, political discussions amongst people or rants like this through books or social media — then the ones in power would only paint a picture that would tell that this country is the greatest and there is no problem whatsoever. So, please do pinpoint problems, be skeptical, don't easily give into jingoism — where you need to thump your chest and bat your eyes away, whenever someone says we have a major problem in this country.

I am quoting the nationally accepted man of philosophical brilliance — Gandhi Ji.

'Be the change, you want to see!'

I am the change that I want to see in the society; I am discarding all the bullshit we have conveniently accepted to

142

cover up some weird Indian heritage and cultural ethics; I am discarding every evil I see. Maybe I am not a selfless social worker or a revolutionary or have political ambitions but I am the change I want to see. I am doing my bit not to be a bad citizen of this country; to at least help others to understand what changes I am talking about or just open a discussion (not mindless arguments). I am an armchair activist; I talk about the problems of my country; I praise my country for all the good it upholds; I am a proud Indian — but that doesn't mean I am a blind patriot. People in power want jingoism and blind patriotism, so that no one question why problems of our country aren't solved? If patriotism establishes that calling on bullshit is bullshit, then it's quite counterproductive to be overly patriotic. Patriotism is when the freedom fighters of our country addressed a problem — colonialism by Britishers — that's patriotism of highest order. To say there is a problem and bringing it to the realm of civil and participative discussion is what patriotism is about. People who are too stupid and blind to say that we are the greatest, are the ones who don't want a better life and engage in reality — where they can say — okay our country is not the greatest in the world but let's find why it isn't and what we can do to make it the greatest in the world? Here, that's patriotism for you! Please, don't tell me that when you go out to enjoy a movie — and the national anthem is played at the beginning — it is patriotism — it's bullshit and forced conditioning of jingoism. If you want to give a patriotic message, then please play a message not to throw garbage outside or education is the key for this country's success or anything which conveys a necessary social message — that would be a real constructive conditioning. National anthem created by the legendary scholar Rabindranath Tagore is so beautiful and auspicious, that it is reserved when we as a country are celebrating something major — maybe Indians winning International laurels or it is the Independence day. The national anthem isn't a joke or a tool that should be blatantly used for forced patriotism. It has a gravitas that is far serious and important in its tone — it is meant to give collective consciousness to people on moments of national pride; it shouldn't be made fun of or belittled by playing it before a movie in cinema halls. To question something is a virtue and to blindly follow or just ignore a problem is moronic and stupid.

About the Author

Anushray Singh is a civil engineer, writer and a filmmaker. He has completed his engineering at the coveted VIT University, Vellore in 2017 and is enroute becoming a professional writer and a filmmaker. He has a penchant for writing blogs, short stories, articles and flash fiction regarding psychology, philosophy, social issues and filmmaking. He has also created numerous short films, visual poems and travel documentaries. He also carries an experience in media production and management. He currently lives in Noida. In India: Everything is Sunshine and Rainbow is his first book.

www.ingramcontent.com/pod-product-compliance
Lightning Source LLC
Chambersburg PA
CBHW062058270326
41931CB00013B/3126